What would YOU DO?

JOHN QUIÑONES

ALSO BY JOHN QUIÑONES:

Heroes Among Us: Ordinary People, Extraordinary Choices

What would YOU DO?

WORDS OF WISDOM ABOUT DOING THE RIGHT THING

JOHN QUIÑONES

 KINGSWELL

Los Angeles • New York

Published by Kingswell, an imprint of Disney Book Group. No part of this book may be reproduced or transmitted in any form or by any means, electronic or mechanical, including photocopying, recording, or by any information storage and retrieval system, without written permission from the publisher.

For information address Kingswell,
1101 Flower Street, Glendale, California 91201.

Library of Congress Cataloging-in-Publication Data

Quiñones, John.
  What would you do? : words of wisdom about doing the right thing / John Quiñones.
    pages cm. -- (What would you do?)
    ISBN 978-1-4847-2620-4 (hardback)
1. Conduct of life. 2. Ethics. 3. Quiñones, John. I. Title.
  BJ1589.Q56 2015
  170'.44--dc23
                            2014045232

First Hardcover Edition, May 2015
10 9 8 7 6 5 4 3 2 1

G475-5664-5-15079
Printed in the United States of America

Editorial Director: Wendy Lefkon
Executive Editor: Laura Hopper

SUSTAINABLE FORESTRY INITIATIVE   Certified Sourcing
www.sfiprogram.org
SFI-00993

THIS LABEL APPLIES TO TEXT STOCK

ACKNOWLEDGMENTS

❦

Hosting *What Would You Do?* is a lot like holding up a mirror to human behavior. The reflection we see is sometimes heartbreaking. But when everyday heroes step up, it warms the heart and restores our faith in humankind.

So my first thanks go out to those amazing people who walk—unsuspectingly—into our scenarios and, after witnessing abuse and injustice, choose to raise their voices in protest. They give the rest of us hope for a better world.

It's been said that life is only as good as the family you have. I thank my parents, Bruno and Maria, and my sisters, Irma and Rosemary, for planting those early moral and ethical seeds that helped me become the man that I am. I certainly didn't always follow their sage advice, but today it allows me to shine a light on and cherish honorable behavior when I witness it in others.

I now have my own loving and caring family: my wonderful sons, Julian and Nicco, my lovely daughter, Andrea, and my beautiful wife, Deanna. Thanks for your patience, for all those ideas for new *WWYD* scenarios, and for the incredible compassion you show daily for your fellow man, woman, and child. You inspire me.

It takes a small village to produce our broadcasts. We could not do it—for eight years running now—without the undying support of Ben Sherwood, the co-president of Disney/ABC Television Group, and James Goldston, the president of the ABC News division. Thank you for allowing us the opportunity to produce a show that continues to make such a difference in people's lives.

Every *WWYD* hour comprises at least five different scenarios, and each segment takes an entire day to film and produce. It's a tall order, and we could not do it without our executive producer, Danielle Rossen, at the helm. She is a bundle of energy and a fountain of innovative ideas. Under her watch, the *WWYD* team scours newspapers, watches countless hours of social media videos, and then brainstorms about new issues and dilemmas that are in the news.

Thanks, too, to David Sloan, my executive producer at *20/20*, who for years oversaw both that dynamic newsmagazine and *WWYD*, providing us with his tremendous guidance and insight.

Behind the scenes, we have a fabulous team of producers and editors who spend weeks—sometimes months—molding each *WWYD* scenario. Our senior producer, Lee Hoffman, is a veteran television journalist—and an excellent writer—who breathes fresh air into our *WWYD* scripts.

A massive thank you to Erica Butler, *WWYD*'s development and production manager—the young woman who oversees all our elaborate and often complicated shoots. She helps the operation hum along like a well-oiled machine.

There is no way we could capture all the *WWYD* magic without those cameras and microphones so creatively hidden in ketchup and mustard bottles, on bookshelves, on ceilings, and behind mirrors. The masters of it all: a production company called TV Boy, run by Nick Skolnick, Chris Morgan, Michael Bergman, and James diPretoro. Their technicians—always operating behind the scenes—not only capture every memorable *WWYD* word and reaction; they are an absolute joy to work with.

Always by my side are the digital video crews that "break" each and every scene with me—with their cameras out in the open—once we've witnessed the bystanders' reactions. Tony Pagano, Lincoln Wiese, Rick Juliano, and Richie Tropiano have spent thousands of hours hiding with me in kitchens, closets, vacant warehouses, and vans, waiting for the right moment to emerge into view with the comforting words "This has all been part of *What Would You Do?*" They provide the show with much more than excellent video and sound: they suggest different twists and turns for our scenarios and even lines for our actors.

The one person who's been on the show longer than anyone except me, is our security guard, Bobby Ramos. This former New York City police officer is always sitting in the middle of the action, incognito, making sure things don't get out of hand. The entire "behind-the-scenes" team has become a real family. And, I can't imagine doing the show without them. Thanks, too, to my tremendously bright and hardworking assistant, Laura Ramirez, who not only coordinates all my work at *ABC News* and *WWYD* but also works on stories for *20/20*, often in two languages—English and Spanish. ¡Gracias!

My gratitude also goes out to Kingswell editorial director Wendy Lefkon and Kingswell executive editor Laura Hopper, who made the entire process of writing this book a real joy.

And above all, thanks to Jennifer Cohen, my literary agent, who approached me at a sidewalk café on New York City's Columbus Avenue a couple of years ago and insisted that this book be written. She just wouldn't take no for an answer. Her creative guidance—and friendship—made writing this book a wonderful experience.

Big thanks to my agents Jay Sures and Ryan Hayden at United Talent Agency and my manager, Gordon Gilbertson, at Gilbertson Entertainment. You guys are a tremendous source of wisdom and support.

Finally, thanks to our millions of viewers throughout the country and all over the world, who have tuned in to make *WWYD* such a huge success. We promise to come up with even more novel scenarios and ideas that will keep all of you entertained but, above all, on your toes and on your best behavior.

INTRODUCTION

☙ ❧

Our prime purpose in this life is to help others. And if you can't help them, at least don't hurt them. Be kind whenever possible. It is always possible.

—Dalai Lama

I will never forget the journey I took several years ago through the Himalayas along the border between India and Tibet. I was on assignment for ABC News, and it was there, in those majestic, cloud-shrouded mountains, that I had the honor of interviewing the great Buddhist leader, the Dalai Lama.

"What is the secret to true happiness?" I asked him. He paused for a moment and then responded in a whisper, calm and peaceful. "The development of compassion and understanding for others," he explained. "It's the only thing that can bring us the tranquility and happiness we all seek."

Those simple words pretty well explain the whole concept behind

What Would You Do?, the TV show I created and have hosted for almost a decade. With hidden cameras and actors, we have staged hundreds of scenarios, forcing unsuspecting people to decide what to do when they witness something rude, troubling, or bothersome.

Many of our ideas are ripped right from the headlines. The situation can be as simple as someone texting incessantly on their cell phone at dinner or a teenager yelling at his mother.

The most memorable scenarios are the ones that dig a little deeper. What do you do if you see someone stealing a waiter's tip at a restaurant or spanking their young child violently at the grocery store?

Or—and more to the Dalai Lama's point—what if, right in front of you, someone is being ridiculed for being poor or disabled or gay? What if someone is being discriminated against because of his or her religion, skin color, or accent?

It happens every second of every day all over the world. And it affords us a great opportunity to take measure of true character.

When you come face-to-face with abuse or injustice and that little voice in the back of your head says, "*Do* something," do you step in, or do you step away?

Since *WWYD*'s premier, I, like a fly on the wall, have watched every single one of our scenarios unfold. It's the ultimate "reality" show and it has been fascinating to witness. Some people choose not to get involved because they are either too shy or scared or they simply don't care. Others clearly *want* to speak up—you can see it on their faces—but Something holds them back.

But there are always the everyday heroes who come along and

step in valiantly—often at risk to themselves—to defend the targets of hatred or bigotry or abuse. And they do so eloquently and with great compassion. Like a human GPS system, they guide us down the path toward the kindest, most inspiring moral and ethical behavior.

This book is a collection of the valuable lessons I've learned from all those years of conducting our *WWYD* laboratory of human behavior. The issues we showcase occur every day in America. In fact, the issues occur in most of the world. But they happen mostly in the shadows, when we think no one is watching or listening. We at *WWYD* have simply chosen to shine a light on them.

The results are so fascinating and revealing that today schools and universities throughout the country use our *WWYD* segments in their psychology and sociology classes.

Virtually every day I get e-mails and tweets from fans of the show telling me, "John, I had a *What Would You Do?* moment today! Where were you?!!"

Maybe this would indeed be a better world if we all thought those *WWYD* cameras were always rolling, constantly monitoring our behavior, like a moral compass. If we knew that someone else might be watching, we would be on our best behavior. We would pay more attention to the bullying, discrimination, and injustice that too often surrounds us. It would be a powerful reminder that all of us can afford to be a little more understanding, caring, and compassionate.

Most certainly we would be more enlightened.

WHERE IT ALL BEGAN

⋘ ⋙

What would you do if you were a shy, scrawny little dark-skinned boy who lived in poverty, and because of that, the odds of "making it" in the world seemed stacked against you? Well, you would dream big dreams.

And that is exactly what I did growing up in the barrios of San Antonio, Texas. Back then there wasn't much else my family could afford to do *but* dream. And since I was a very curious and adventurous character, I would always fantasize about someday traveling the world, meeting fascinating people and telling their stories.

Well, for more than thirty years, that is exactly what I have had the privilege of doing for ABC News. It's been the greatest job in the world. As a network correspondent, I've had a front row seat to some amazing world events. I've covered everything from wars in Central America and the Middle East, to the American space program, to the disappearing rain forests in the Amazon and Africa. I've interviewed everyone from Fidel Castro to Jane Goodall.

I have traveled to virtually every country on the planet. And along the way, I have witnessed firsthand both the good and the bad people can do to each other. As a reporter, I have challenged evildoers and celebrated heroes.

I guess you can say that, in many ways, I have been studying and training for *What Would You Do?* my entire life.

MY MOTHER, MARIA

CB 80

Our very first influences in life—and usually the most powerful—are our parents. Good or bad, they set the stage for our moral and ethical behavior in those early, formative years.

And so it was in my case. My sisters and I had an exceptional mother, Maria Garcia Quiñones, who, without a doubt, was solely responsible for planting those *What Would You Do?* ideas in my young, curious brain so many years ago.

Maria was the most loving, caring, sensitive person I have ever known. She didn't have much formal education—she had to drop out of school in the eighth grade to help support her family—but in my eyes, she had a doctorate in love, empathy, and social responsibility.

Our small two-bedroom home on the poor side of the tracks in San Antonio was a lifesaving haven for abused women, runaway kids, even stray dogs and cats. No one in trouble or need was turned away. Maybe it was because she, herself, had suffered poverty and discrimination. Or maybe it was a result of her strong Catholic upbringing. Whatever it was, Maria could connect with and relate to victims of all kinds of misfortune and injustice. And she did it by simply following the Golden Rule: Treat others the way you would want to be treated yourself.

My mother worked very hard cleaning the homes of rich folks on the north side of San Antonio. As a housemaid, she was paid twenty dollars a day. Of course, she couldn't afford a babysitter, so while my older sister, Irma, was at school, my little sister, Rosemary, and I would jump on a city bus and go to work with my mom.

Back at our own little two-bedroom bungalow on Arizona Street, Maria cooked every single meal, washed our clothes, and kept the place as tidy as possible. Every night, after my father got home from work—he earned fifty dollars a week, first as a tree trimmer with the Asplundh tree company, and then as a janitor—we all had dinner, together. We didn't have much in material goods, but we were tremendously rich with the blessings of love and family.

Maria was an incredibly compassionate, giving person. Whenever anyone would turn up on our doorstep in need of a meal or a shoulder to cry on, she would turn to my sisters and me and ask, "If you were in the same shoes, what would you do?" *¿Qué harias tu?*

I would like to think that her concern for fellow human beings rubbed off on her son—the kid who dreamed of someday becoming a journalist.

Today, as a network correspondent, I frequently interview people who have suffered loss and heartache—the victims of domestic violence, war, or natural disasters—and I always try to put myself in their shoes. That always leads to a better understanding of someone's plight and, in the end, a truer, more complete story for the viewer.

"*¿Qué harias tu?*"—*What would you do?* I wonder if my mother had any idea how those four simple words would someday resonate with millions of television viewers and Internet users.

It's an important reminder for all parents and caretakers. Our children are always listening, watching, learning from us. They may not always listen to our advice, but they're constantly absorbing what we *do*.

We should always try our best to lead by good example. *What Would You Do?* is my mother's legacy.

WHEN LIFE GIVES YOU
GREEN BEAN SANDWICHES

C3 8O

I hate to sound like one of those older people complaining about how easy young folks have it today. But believe it or not, I got my first job—stocking groceries—at the age of eight. That's right, eight years old.

It was at a neighborhood store called La Chicanita—the Little Mexican American—and I begged the owner to hire me because I saw how my parents struggled to provide for our family. I wanted to contribute—even if it was with my paltry twenty-five-dollar weekly salary. Plus, I knew I could take one dollar from that to buy my own candy.

I also had another part-time job. At night, my cousin Joe and I shined shoes on the streets of downtown San Antonio. Ten cents a pair. There we were, two pint-sized kids, hitting all the cantinas - the bars - on Guadalupe Street, because we discovered quickly that drunk men were more generous with their tips.

I learned at a very tender age all about responsibility and the value of a dollar.

So when my father, Bruno, was suddenly laid off from his job as a high school janitor in the summer of 1965, I was ready to do whatever I could to help my family get back on their feet. I was thirteen years old.

Like many other Mexican Americans in south Texas, we had one option: migrant farmwork. My mom, my dad, my two sisters, and I joined a caravan of trucks, and with a large group of other migrants, we journeyed 1,600 miles north to Traverse City, Michigan, the "cherry capital of the world."

A couple of days into the trip, somewhere near Indianapolis, our truck got separated from the rest of the caravan. We were lost, and it wasn't long before we ran out of gas and food. The boss man who had contracted us for the farmwork—and had the money for our food—was hundreds of miles ahead of us.

Fortunately, we spotted a Catholic church. I'll never forget my mother knocking on the pastor's office door and, a few minutes later, walking out with a gallon can of green beans, a loaf of bread, and some money for gasoline.

For the next two days, my family survived on green bean sandwiches. I never knew those canned veggies could taste so good.

As soon as we arrived in the cherry orchards of Northport, Michigan, on a peninsula north of Traverse City, we got to work, teetering atop ten-foot ladders, picking the tiny fruit off the trees. We earned seventy-five cents for every gallon bucket we harvested. It took me an hour to fill each of those giant cans.

It was there in northern Michigan—just a few miles from the Canadian border—that I had my first encounter with prejudice and racism. One day, after having picked cherries for weeks in the blistering sun, my dad piled us into our truck and drove thirty miles to the larger town of Traverse City to buy groceries, some clothes at the Goodwill store, and, if there was any money left over, some ice cream.

We had no idea what was in store for us. As soon as we walked into the supermarket, everyone stopped what they were doing and stared at us—this motley crew of Spanish-speaking farmworkers. We were strangers in a very strange land. Store employees followed us around, made snide comments, and made it clear we were not welcome.

I felt belittled and angry. The Quiñones family had been in the United States for seven generations! We were Americans, and yet they ridiculed us and called us *foreigners.*

It made no sense to me. There we were, working hard to make a good, honest living—refusing food stamps or public assistance—and people looked down on us for that?

A few weeks later, we piled back into our truck and drove several hundred miles south, following the harvest to the tomato fields of Swanton, Ohio, just outside Toledo. We were paid thirty-five cents for every large basket of tomatoes we picked. And here I excelled, filling up one hundred bushels a day.

I'll never forget one particular morning in Swanton. There I was, kneeling on the cold, wet ground at six in the morning, staring at rows of tomato plants that looked to me like they went on for miles and miles. That was what I had to look forward to that day.

My father, who had spent most of his boyhood picking cotton in south Texas, looked down at me and said, "Think about it, Juanito. Do you really want to do this kind of work for the rest of your life? Or do you want a college education?"

It was a no-brainer. I certainly knew I didn't want to do *that* kind of backbreaking work for the rest of my life. I promised myself right then and there that I would do everything in my power to get to college someday.

Those tomato fields, the hard work, the prejudice, and, yes, even those green bean sandwiches propelled me to a rock-solid determination to make something better of myself.

I know it sounds crazy, but everyone should be so lucky.

NEVER GIVE UP HOPE

Cʒ ʃɔ

Life can be a tough struggle—especially when you start off at a disadvantage. You're born into poverty, or with a physical disability, or to a single parent with barely enough time and energy to put food on the table. And then, because of any or all of that, you're the target of ridicule and bullying.

That's when the going gets really tough.

How in the world can you aspire to bigger and better things when it seems the odds are stacked against you? How do you keep your chin up when you feel all alone and there's no one to lend a helping hand?

I know the feeling. When I was a child, we were so poor I had to wear the same clothes to school every other day. I had to endure the stares of kids who made fun of me because all I brought for lunch were bean-and-tortilla tacos while most of the other kids had their fancy white bread and bologna.

Again, it was my mother, Maria, to the rescue. She constantly reminded my sisters and me that it didn't matter on what side of town we were born. She would get very animated and point to my head.

"What really matters is what's in here . . . in your brain," she would say. And then, pointing to my chest, she would add, "What matters is what's here . . . in your *corazón*—your heart."

Those little reminders gave me hope, but I was still incredibly frustrated—and often felt defeated—by all the negative messages the rest of society kept sending my way. When I was a teenager, reading the local newspapers or watching TV news, it seemed like there was nothing but bad news about Latinos. Anyone reading or watching from outside our community would get the idea that we were all illegal immigrants, members of street gangs, and criminals and drug dealers.

Now, don't get me wrong. The west side of San Antonio was a scary place to grow up back in the 1960s and '70s. Several of my classmates were stabbed to death because they happened to walk through a rival gang's turf. Three of my own cousins were heroin addicts and drug dealers who spent most of their lives in federal prison. So it was no surprise that society as a whole kept presuming and expecting the worst of us.

But I knew there were also many positive stories to be told about Hispanics in my neighborhood and, for that matter, in the barrios all across America. Stories about our strong work ethic, our love of family, our entrepreneurial spirit—all *American* success stories.

And I knew just the right person to tell those stories. At the age of thirteen, I dreamed of someday becoming a television reporter. Yet it was tough to visualize that dream, because there were very few Hispanic faces on television—hardly anyone who looked like me.

In fact, no one—except my parents—believed that I could even make it to college. In middle school, whenever I asked my counselors about college prep courses, they would say, "It's wonderful that you have such great dreams, John. But we think you should enroll in vocational courses like metal and wood shop. Maybe auto mechanics."

There's nothing wrong with those trades. Many people make a good, hard living doing that kind of work. But I wanted to go to college, and my own counselors—the very people who are supposed to encourage students—kept dissuading me, telling me I would probably never make it in college.

I endured the same kind of reactions and biases we often get when we stage our scenarios on *WWYD*: people judging each other by the color of their skin and the accent in their speech.

It was defeating and depressing. Several times I was so down that I considered dropping out of school.

But then, one day, in the hallways of Jeremiah Rhodes Junior High, I met Louie Rodriguez, a recent immigrant from Mexico. Louie lived in public housing; his family was barely scraping by. And his Mexican accent was even stronger than mine. But to hear Louie talk, he—and I—was destined for success and greatness. He was the lone voice of positivity in a world where everyone else was telling us we would never amount to much. Louie became my best friend.

Whenever I felt down and out, there he was, always pushing me to carry on, always seeing the glass not as half empty but as half full. I can still hear his wonderfully optimistic voice: "We can do it, Johnny. I *know* we can!"

It was Louie who first came up with the idea that instead of going to the high school in our neighborhood, where virtually all the students were Latino, we should enroll at Brackenridge High—a school that was located outside our district. The students there were much more integrated—Hispanic, African American, and white. The academic standards were also higher there, and we would be forced to perfect our English.

It was also at Brackenridge that we learned about a federal anti-poverty program called Upward Bound. It provided advanced classes to inner-city kids in high school, to improve their chances of getting accepted to college. We signed up for interviews with the program's counselors who were visiting my high school. A few weeks later came the startling but great news that we had been chosen as two of the ten Upward Bound students from my high school.

Today there would be no John Quiñones at ABC News if it had not been for that federal program. Some might call it a government handout. For me—and for Louie, who, after graduating from college, became a successful businessman—Upward Bound was a lifesaver. And so it has been for hundreds of thousands of other high school kids who have soared to new heights with a little push and a helping hand.

The reverend Martin Luther King Jr. once said, "Faith is taking the first step even when you don't see the whole staircase." So true, because after that, you can take another step. Then another.

My advice is simple: Don't listen to those negative messages that society often lobs our way—particularly to people of color. Surround yourself with people who believe in you. Shoot for the stars. Take advantage of every single opportunity you get. And never, never give up.

GET OUT OF THAT SHELL!

$\text{C\!R} \quad \text{\&D}$

Too often in life, we fail before even trying to give it our best shot. We surrender to inner demons that keep us from succeeding.

When I was a kid in school, I was incredibly shy. I was skinny and awkward and spoke with a funny accent, but I had big dreams. I had always wanted to go into broadcast journalism, but I was deathly afraid of speaking in front of an audience. I would perspire, shake, and withdraw into a shell. Not a good thing if you want to someday work in front of the camera.

What got me out of that shell? The almost desperate determination to make my parents proud and to help provide them with a better life. I saw how hard they worked and witnessed the sacrifices they made for me and my two sisters. I felt a deep responsibility to make life just a little bit easier for them. I knew I could do that by excelling in school, college, and, someday, a successful profession.

To achieve any of that, I would first have to conquer my greatest fears and insecurities.

So in middle school, I joined the drama class. And then I took things a bit further and tried out for the role of Romeo in *Romeo and Juliet*. Sure, I was a nervous wreck, but I was also determined to prove to the world that I was capable of much more than what was expected of me. So before my audition, I went for a long run. At the advice of my drama teacher, I took deep breaths and practiced a little yoga. I visualized myself as the best Romeo there ever was. It didn't hurt that Mary Lou Gomez, the pretty girl playing Juliet, was an accomplished actress who, for some reason, took a liking to me. Behind the curtain, before we went onstage, she grabbed me by the cheeks, kissed me, and then simply said, "Now, let's just go out there and do this!"

Well, I got the part. The good news was that I would get to kiss Mary Lou again, onstage. The bad news was that, in my very macho school, I had to wear a leotard. I can still hear the catcalls and whistles I got when I took the stage. I'm so glad YouTube did not exist back then. That video would have gone viral.

But by forcing myself to get out there and perform before hundreds of my fellow students, I quickly overcame my timidness and stage fright. I learned to slow down my rapid-fire speech, enunciate, and deliver my lines loud enough for the audience in the last rows of the auditorium to hear.

The simple decision to stand up straight, take a deep breath, and give it my best shot on that stage forever changed my life. I gained a renewed sense of self, courage, and confidence. The deeper source of it was the advice and encouragement from my acting coach—a woman who recognized a spark of talent in me. It also came from the positive energy I got from my fellow actors. And, of course, the applause I received from the audience. For the first time in my life, I felt validated. A new John Quiñones emerged into the light. From that moment on, nothing and no one could hold me back.

Everyone—it's never too early or too late—should force themselves to stand tall before an audience and deliver their message. The key? Find just *one* person in the crowd and focus on them. Try not to read from a script. Speak from your heart. It helps if you have a particular passion for your subject. Then breathe, smile, and go for it . . . in a loud, clear fashion.

Intimidating? Of course. But the payoff of newfound self-esteem and renewed confidence is immeasurable.

MAKE YOUR OWN GOOD LUCK

CR 8O

I was accepted to St. Mary's University in San Antonio, thanks to those college prep courses at Upward Bound. But, of course, my parents had no money for my tuition, so I had to rely on student loans and grants from the government. As a freshman, I also held down three part-time jobs. I worked in the school cafeteria and in the geology department sorting rocks. And at night I was a drugstore deliveryman for Blanco Pharmacy, driving an old beat-up Volkswagen, delivering prescription medicine to little old ladies.

I always had to be careful when I told folks, "I deliver drugs," because, of course, they'd presume the worst. You know, that whole Latino-drug-dealer stereotype.

I was eighteen years old and earning very little money, but between my deliveries I had the chance to practice my "newsman's voice." I would sit in the men's room at the pharmacy and read newspaper stories into a little tape recorder and then play the recording back over and over again.

One night, Richard Teniente, the owner of the pharmacy, was

standing outside the bathroom door when he heard me reading.

"You really want to go into broadcasting, don't you?" he asked. "I think I might be able to help you."

It turned out Mr. Teniente knew a group of Mexican American activists who called themselves the Bilingual Bicultural Coalition on the Mass Media, or the BBC.

Angry that radio and television stations in San Antonio had hardly any Hispanic reporters on the air—even though the population of the city was 60 percent Latino—the BBC started protesting outside the stations' studios. They pointed to the Communications Act of 1934, which said that the airwaves in this country belonged not to private corporations but to the American public. Employees of broadcast stations should therefore reflect the ethnic makeup of their audience.

With their loud protests and picket signs, the BBC threatened to ask the federal government to revoke the stations' broadcast licenses. And that freaked out the management at every radio and TV station in San Antonio. They started hiring any young Hispanic with a decent voice.

And there I was, reading my copy in a drugstore men's room.

Mr. Teniente told me he knew the general manager of a local radio station. That was all I needed to hear. For weeks, I kept harassing him to get me an introduction, which he finally did.

And that led to an internship at KKYX radio. Now, mind you, as a typical college student, I was a fan of rock music and R & B. KKYX was a *country* music station. But of course I wasn't going to pass this up. It was the kind of break I had been dreaming about for years. (And by the way, I grew to love country music.)

I was hired and paid two dollars an hour at KKYX, which was located in the Texas hill country, about twenty miles outside San Antonio. And what were my duties in my first job in broadcasting? Well, you might have to be from Texas to understand this, but the disc jockeys at the station had horses they rode in rodeos, parades, and public appearances. They were kept in the back of the studios. My job as an intern included feeding and cleaning up after those horses!

But late at night, I would sneak into the audio booths at the station and record my voice, reading whatever I could get my hands on. Over and over again. I would spend hours in there, working on my diction and pronunciation.

The only problem was that at that hour, there was no one at the station to critique my work except the janitor. His name was Pablo. He was a wonderful Latino who spoke very little English.

"How does it sound?" I would ask.

"Mas o menos," he would say. "More or less, it sounds okay."

After months of practice, I had the station manager listen to my recordings. He liked them, and he asked me to tape a local tag to a nationally produced commercial (voiced by a real announcer). Just the tag.

These were the first words ever spoken on broadcast radio by John Quiñones: "Now available at Walgreens in San Antonio." That's it. All three seconds of it.

But I was so excited. I called all my cousins, aunts, and uncles and told everyone, "You have to listen at 1:12 this afternoon. But you'll have to listen carefully or you'll miss it!"

And then, a few months later, the station manager let me do the news on Sunday nights. Well, it was actually Monday mornings, between one and three. Five minutes of news, on the air.

I think we had a total of four listeners: my mom and dad and two sisters.

But it was a start. And that's the way it should be. At the beginning of any career, we all make mistakes. I can't tell you the number of times I introduced a taped report from a reporter in the field only to find out that the tape machine refused to play it. Or times I didn't get to read my news copy in advance and, live on the air, came upon a word that I couldn't pronounce. I verbally stumbled all over it. Or times when I suddenly got a case of the giggles while reading the news. I would have to push the mute button . . . and subject our listeners to what seemed like an eternity of dead air.

In broadcasting, you want to make sure those blunders are on local radio somewhere . . . not on national television.

After about a year, I was offered a full-time job as a newsreader at another radio station. And my career was off and running.

Lucky break? Yes, certainly at the very beginning.

But when you get a lucky break, you grab that opportunity and run with it. You keep working relentlessly toward perfection and excellence.

Of course, you will stumble, but you pick yourself up and do it again and again.

You need to keep trying to make your own good luck—even when your job is to clean up poop and your only critic is the janitor.

IT HAS TO BE MORE THAN A
DREAM—ENTERPRISE

CB BO

It is one thing to dream big dreams. But making them come true takes more than wishing and praying and fantasizing. It takes persistence, determination, hard work, and ingenuity. It means never taking your eyes off the prize.

I was pretty happy to get my start at local radio stations in Texas, but as I've said, I always wanted to be a *television* reporter. I could see the power of the camera, film, and video in journalism. As a teenager, I spent hours watching the greats of network news: Walter Cronkite, Peter Jennings, Barbara Walters, Tom Brokaw. I loved the sense of adventure that came with their work, covering wars and natural disasters, reporting from far-off and exotic locations.

But no one inspired me like Geraldo Rivera, the cool investigative reporter on *20/20* and, later, his own show, *Good Night America*, a precursor to ABC's *Nightline*. He had long hair and that trademark mustache, often wore jeans, and just dove into the kind of stories no one else dared to cover. He was exposing injustice and corruption in a bold, brash way and making a real difference in people's lives.

Television news had never seen anyone like Geraldo. And because Geraldo had a Hispanic last name, being half Puerto Rican, he was the only one in network news I could relate to. I wanted to be just like him.

Of course, I was just starting out. There wasn't a single frame of me on video, so back home in Texas, no one in TV news would take a chance on me. My future looked pretty bleak. I was earning very little money—just eight hundred dollars a month. I remember that, to supplement my income, KTRH radio in Houston paid me fifty dollars a month to buy gasoline for my company car. Many times, I had to use that money to buy groceries and pray I wouldn't run out of gas!

I was about ready to give up on journalism altogether and try something else, maybe the legal profession. I filled out an application to the University of Houston law school. But it's funny how life is. At one of my last auditions for a TV job, I met Merimil Rodriguez, a Puerto Rican newspaper reporter with a master's degree from the Columbia University Graduate School of Journalism. I shared with her my frustrations and my plans to leave broadcasting.

"I can see that you have such a passion for journalism," she said. "Why are you applying to law school? If you're going back to school, why not enroll in the best journalism program in the world, Columbia?"

Columbia? That lofty Ivy League school in New York City? It was a great idea, but my chances of getting accepted to such a prestigious institution were pretty slim—or so I thought.

Still, I went for it. I filled out the application and wrote two essays about my life and aspirations. And I included a letter of recommendation from Merimil Rodriguez, the Columbia alum I befriended at that chance meeting in Houston.

For the next four months, I checked my mailbox every single day. And then it arrived: a big light blue envelope from Columbia University. I nervously ripped it open, and there it was: my letter of acceptance!

I was beyond ecstatic, but then it hit me: how in the world was I going to pay the tuition?

I booked the cheapest overnight flight I could get to New York City and started knocking on every financial aid door I could find at Columbia. I begged and I pleaded, promising to work my tail off and make the school proud.

It paid off. A month later, I was awarded a fellowship from NBC News, which covered my tuition, books, and living expenses.

I couldn't believe it. This Mexican American kid who had once spoken no English and had grown up shining shoes and picking tomatoes was on his way to graduate school.

That summer, I packed up a U-Haul trailer and drove all the way from Houston to the upper west side of Manhattan.

I absolutely loved New York and its beautiful mosaic of people. Back home in San Antonio, you were black, white, or Mexican American—everyone relegated to their own segregated corner of the city. And the three groups seldom interacted.

But in New York, I quickly made friends with Jewish, Muslim, and Asian students. And guess what? They accepted me. They actually found me interesting . . . unique and exotic. For the first time, I didn't feel like an outsider in my own country.

It was at Columbia that I learned one of my most important lessons about taking advantage of every single opportunity you get to make your dreams come true.

One Monday night, our guest lecturer was Richard Salant, the president of CBS News.

I thought, "This might be my one and only opportunity to come face-to-face with such a powerful force in network news." So after his talk, I nervously approached Mr. Salant, introduced myself, and asked if I might be able to interview him for my class thesis. That was only part of why I wanted to speak with him. I was about to graduate from Columbia. I would soon need a job. And I really just wanted to hand him my resume.

"Sure," he said. "Just call my assistant at CBS and set it up."

The next day, I called Mr. Salant's assistant and she scheduled an appointment for two weeks later.

I showed up half an hour early at the CBS studios on Fifty-Seventh Street in New York. I was a bundle of nerves. You see, back then CBS was considered the cream of the crop of the network news divisions. I was in awe as I was ushered down a hallway past the portraits of Edward R. Murrow, Walter Cronkite, Mike Wallace, and Dan Rather—all broadcast news legends.

As soon as I was taken into Mr. Salant's office, I started asking my questions about TV news. It was all over in less than fifteen minutes. Then I stood up, shook Mr. Salant's hand, reached into my breast pocket, and pulled out my little resume.

"By the way," I told him, "I'm graduating in May and would love to work for CBS News."

Mr. Salant just smiled and shook his head. I had no idea what he was thinking. Not only was Mr. Salant the president of CBS News; he was also a lawyer. And he played his cards close to his vest. Was he angry? Was he impressed? Had I just blown my chances of ever working for the network?

I found out two days later, when I got a call from John Lane, one of the vice presidents of CBS News. "The president of the division just forwarded me your resume and said I should meet with you. He describes you as a very 'enterprising' young man."

Two weeks later, I was on my way to Chicago to audition for a job as a reporter for WBBM-TV, the local CBS station. And I nailed it.

The kid who had been rejected by just about every TV station in Texas was hired as a reporter in one of the largest television markets in the country.

All because of what my Jewish friends would call chutzpah. My Latino friends call it *ganas*—the unbelievable audacity to shoot for the stars in pursuit of a dream.

The lesson: take advantage of every single opportunity you get and capitalize on every chance meeting.

TAKE ADVANTAGE OF ALL YOUR STRENGTHS

CR 80

Each one of us is unique. There is almost always something we can do that gives us an advantage over others. It's either a part of our DNA or a result of how we were raised. It could be anything: a physical strength, a facility with math and sciences, or the kind of compassion that makes you a perfect candidate for the medical field.

Whatever it is, we should always take full advantage of our special attributes—no matter what trade or profession we pursue.

The "edge" I capitalized on and brought to television news was being Latino and being able to speak fluent Spanish. There was a dire need for that in a nation where Hispanics were about to become the largest minority.

As a teenager in San Antonio, I noticed that the only stories on television about the Latino community that ever made the evening news were reports about crime, drugs, gangs, and illegal immigration. I knew there were many more, positive stories that could be told about my community, but no one would cover them—in large part because there were hardly any Hispanic reporters on the air.

When I finally got my big break, I vowed to change that. I knew that because of where I came from and my ability to speak both English and Spanish, I had a golden opportunity to shine the light of journalism on those stories that were being overlooked.

The results were almost immediate. The first Emmy Award I received was for a story for WBBM TV in Chicago, in which I posed as an undocumented Mexican worker. I was hired as a foreign correspondent at ABC News, because Central America was erupting in civil war and the network needed someone who spoke Spanish to cover the region.

I was offered my dream position as a correspondent on *Primetime Live* and *20/20* because of my reporting from Colombia, the Amazon, and the Dominican Republic, stories that earned me three more national Emmy Awards.

Of course, I have never been limited to covering just those stories and have never wanted to be defined as ABC's "Hispanic reporter." I'm a reporter who just happens to be Hispanic.

Having said that, it's always wise to capitalize on whatever strengths we can bring to the table.

Like the time a few years ago when thirty-three men were trapped in a gold and copper mine in Copiapó, Chile. They spent sixty-nine days buried half a mile beneath the earth before they were finally rescued and shuttled to the surface. All of them miraculously survived.

It was a huge story and ABC producer Bert Rudman and I were among the two thousand foreign journalists covering it, jockeying for the first interview with a survivor.

We scored the scoop and got the exclusive with miner Mario Sepulveda, mostly because I not only spoke the language but also understood the mannerisms and the local customs. I knew when to push . . . but not push too hard. I knew we had to treat Mario and his family with the utmost respect.

You have to know what you know and then use it to your greatest advantage.

GIVING A VOICE TO THE VOICELESS

 CR ꙮ

When I first joined ABC News as a rookie correspondent in the 1980s, I was assigned to cover the civil wars in Central America. One reason I was hired was that I spoke Spanish. The irony didn't escape me. This was the same guy who used to get punished in school as a kid for speaking Spanish. As a child, the thing that made me feel different seemed like such a liability. But ultimately, as I entered the professional world, it proved to be my greatest strength. Speaking Spanish got me my dream job in network news.

One of my first big stories for ABC was going to be an exclusive interview with the president of Nicaragua, Daniel Ortega. At least, that was what I had been promised by the president's staff. I called Peter Jennings, our *World News Tonight* anchor in New York, to share the good news. Everyone at the network was excited.

And then I got a phone call from Mr. Ortega's office. The president had changed his mind and was canceling the interview. I was petrified. Now I had to call New York with the bad news. It was late in the day, and *World News* would have to revamp its entire newscast, all because I wasn't able to deliver what I had promised. Worst of all, I had to speak to Peter Jennings himself. And this guy was like James Bond: cool, aloof, intimidating.

I expected Mr. Jennings to yell at me or, worse, fire me. After I nervously rattled off my apologies, Mr. Jennings, the 007 of network news, took an audible drag off his cigarette and then calmly delivered words I will never forget.

"Young man," he said, "don't beat yourself up over this. It will likely happen to you again in your career as a correspondent. Promises are made and then broken. Besides, you shouldn't worry so much about talking to presidents and politicians, the movers and shakers of the world. Concentrate more on talking to the moved and the shaken."

He went on to explain that I should take advantage of the fact that, because I'm Latino, I could venture into the most remote corners of Latin America, where I would not be perceived as a "foreigner." Because I could blend into the local population, I had a unique opportunity to interview farmers, peasants, and the children of Central America and South America—the very real victims of war, natural disasters, and poverty. The people often ignored by the media. In many ways, they were the more important story.

Presidents, ambassadors, politicians, the heads of corporations—they can easily gather the press and get their message out, whatever it might be.

"The *campesinos*," said Peter, "they don't have that luxury."

I vowed then and there that I would make it my life's mission to give a voice to those who have none.

Always capitalize on your unique talents, those characteristics that set you apart from the pack. The result will be a product that is unequaled. Because if it comes from your singular heart and mind, then no one in the world can design and deliver it the same way. It is uniquely yours. It doesn't matter if it's some new invention or a television news story.

THE WWYD PHILOSOPHY

CS 80

I have been blessed with an incredibly fascinating journey in journalism, far exceeding my wildest dreams. I have traveled far and wide and interviewed everyone from royal princes and princesses who live in Indian castles to abandoned children who live in the sewers of Bogotá, Colombia.

Along the way, I've had my share of highs and lows, the kinds of successes and pitfalls we all experience in our personal lives and careers. But I have managed to squeeze every ounce of joy from even the most difficult situations, thanks to those three words I heard from my mother when I was a little boy: *"¿Qué harias tu?"—What would you do?* It's what I like to call the WWYD philosophy.

Too often, as we go about our crazy, busy days, we forget what a difference a simple smile or a "How are you doing?" greeting might make to a stranger. It's something we can do every single day, and it costs us nothing.

Of course, it's all the better when we deliver some comforting words to someone in distress or lend a helping hand to someone in need.

We have all been there. You're out shopping or taking a stroll in the park or about to watch a movie, and suddenly, something disturbing happens right in front of you. And that little voice in the back of your head says, "*Do* something!" Do you step in or step away?

The idea for a TV show based on the concept was proposed in 2005 by Chris Whipple, a good friend of mine and a creative and talented producer on ABC's *Primetime Live* and *20/20*. We were both fans of the "Ethicist" column in the *New York Times Magazine*. Randy Cohen wrote about the ethical dilemmas we all face in our daily lives.

"There must be some way to bring these ethical dilemmas to life on television," Chris told me one day in my office.

He had already stumbled upon a compelling real-life scenario: "I kept hearing stories, mostly from mothers of young children, about something they encountered all too often in New York City playgrounds and parks: they would see babysitters mistreating the young children they were supposed to be caring for—ignoring them, verbally abusing them, or worse. These mothers were horrified— and also terribly conflicted about what to do. Would stepping in to confront the babysitter solve the problem? Or would it anger her so much that she might take it out on the child, making matters worse? One woman was so determined to blow the whistle on what she was seeing that she surreptitiously followed the babysitter home, wrote a note to the child's parents, and slipped it to the doorman when the sitter was out of sight."

Fittingly, this was the first ethical dilemma we re-created, with actors and hidden cameras, for a double segment of *Primetime Live*.

At a park in New Jersey, we told our "nanny" to pretend she was totally ignoring a child under her care. The babysitter was busy texting, chatting on her cell, or plugged into her earphones, listening to music. Meanwhile, the child she was supposed to be watching was wandering away, venturing toward danger. What would you do?

The response of passersby was electric—and the variety of ways in which they stepped in to deal with the neglect was fascinating.

Parents at the park quickly confronted the babysitter: "Get off that phone! You have to pay attention to the child you're supposed to be watching!"

And when they realized the nanny wasn't paying attention to them, they got creative. They asked the child, also an actress, for her mommy's phone number and then called the mother. They also wrote notes complaining about the nanny and stuffed them into the child's backpack when the sitter wasn't watching.

Viewers were hooked; the *Columbia Journalism Review* praised the show as a '*Candid Camera* of Ethics,' and these ethical dilemmas would soon become the basis of a new show. When it began its run on Friday nights, *What Would You Do?* dominated the nine p.m. time slot in viewers aged eighteen to forty-nine and toppled *CSI: NY* as the evening's number one network show.

ABC asked for three more hours of the show, then six, and then thirteen hours. To date, we have filmed more than four hundred *WWYD* scenarios, and we're still going strong.

The show resonates with our audience because everyone can relate to it. Every one of us is forced to make these ethical and moral choices every day. But most of the time, they happen behind closed doors, when no one is watching, when no one is listening. With the *What Would You Do?* hidden cameras, we've been able to bring these scenarios—some troubling, some heartwarming, but all fascinating—into the light.

There's no greater feeling for me during our filming than when I come out of hiding and tell people, "This is all part of *What Would You Do?*" There's a huge collective sigh of relief. Laughter, sometimes tears. And we're able to congratulate, celebrate, and relish people's goodness.

Human interaction, that visceral connection, is vital to our happiness. Let's face it, we live in a time when huge institutions have lost their center, when government and politics seem out of control and wars seem endless. The corporations we once relied on change their names and services in a heartbeat. Too many of our heroes have let us down. We're ready to hear some good news, some comfort news, if you will.

What better way to be inspired than by seeing people put aside their fears or preconceived notions and biases to help their fellow man or woman?

And it's even more rewarding when we do it ourselves.

That is why *WWYD* has been such a huge success both on television and all over the world on the Web. It simply *feels* good when we witness people being kind to each other or coming to the aid of a stranger.

Make every day a *WWYD* day. It restores our faith in humanity.

BE THE GOOD SAMARITAN

CB EO

You see a homeless man on the sidewalk. He's dirty, shoeless, begging for a donation. Do you stop and give him a handout, maybe some money or food? Or do you refuse to even make eye contact with him, because you assume he's an alcoholic or a drug addict, and just walk on by?

On *WWYD*, we've done several variations on the theme. And passersby have reacted in both caring and not-so-caring ways.

The most fascinating homeless scenario we filmed was based on the ancient Bible parable "The Good Samaritan." Jesus tells the story of a man who was beaten up by a gang and then was left bleeding on the side of the road. Along came a priest, who saw the man but refused to help. Next came a Levite, who also did nothing—except walk to the other side of the road.

Finally, a Samaritan who was passing through noticed the man. He stopped and bandaged the victim's wounds. He helped him onto his donkey and transported him to a nearby town, where he paid for the man's treatment.

In our *WWYD* scenario, we had several people read that Bible story. They thought it was part of a job interview. We then instructed them to hurry to a nearby building where they would take a test. They had no idea that along the way, they would walk past an actor playing a homeless man begging for help.

Would they stop and help? Or would they hurry on to take that test? Remember, they had just read the story of the Good Samaritan. Interestingly enough, there were several people who clearly saw our homeless man but made no effort to help. But then along came the heroes.

One was a woman who canceled the "interview," and whatever chores she had for the rest of the afternoon, to help our victim.

She even offered to take him to a local clinic to get checked out.

Soon after came an African American man who not only stopped to give advice to our homeless man and console him; he also walked him to a nearby store to buy him some shoes. Later he told me he had been through some tough times himself.

Social psychology experts tell us there are generally two types of people who will step up and help someone in need or defend someone who's being ridiculed. The first group consists of people who have suffered the same type of situation. They can feel the victim's pain because they've been there themselves. The second are those who were raised in a compassionate home. They come to the rescue of someone being victimized because as children they saw their parents doing the same thing for strangers. Time and again, that is what we hear from our heroes. They've "been there" themselves or they were raised right—with a loving, caring heart. That old Good Samaritan story is as relevant today as it was two thousand years ago.

HELPING OTHERS JUST FEELS GOOD

Cʒ ȣͻ

I am constantly surprised and inspired by the people who speak up, step in, and get involved in virtually every one of our *WWYD* scenarios. You can never tell from outside appearances just who will do that. For example, sometimes I'll be watching a scene unfold on hidden camera when some big biker dude with a shaved head and tattoos all over him walks in. I'll say to myself, "No doubt he's going to be the mean racist." But he turns out to be a loving and heroic teddy bear who boldly comes to the rescue of our victim. By the same token, in walks this sweet-looking little old lady with a flower in her hair, and she turns out to be the meanest, crankiest, most biased person of the day!

Our assumptions about people based on their appearances can be terribly wrong. It happened to me often as I was growing up: teachers presuming I wasn't college material, shop owners in Ohio thinking I was about to steal something simply because I was dark-skinned and wore the clothes of a migrant farmworker. Even when I began my career as a local TV reporter, people often presumed I was a member of the camera crew and not the "talent"—simply because they'd never seen a Latino reporter on an English-language TV.

WWYD is all about shattering stereotypes—and so much more. Sociologists tell us that when we help another person out, it also serves to help us. Dr. Caroline Keating, professor of psychology at Colgate University and a consultant to the show, tells me that part of that positive feeling may be our own relief from the tension of empathizing with someone who is in need or in trouble.

"By helping someone, the tension we—and they—experience dissipates," she says. "Helping someone else also pushes our 'self-reward' button—that positive, rewarding feeling we experience after successfully helping someone else."

In other words, when we get involved and help, we ourselves enjoy positive feelings—a sort of 'helper's high.' Our actions confirm that we are good people, thereby enhancing our self-esteem. We realize that we are powerful and in control—after all, we just solved a problem the person we helped couldn't. Often, the person we helped heaps additional reward on us by being grateful, and that makes us look good and feel even better.

On the flip side, Dr. Keating points out that our good deeds sometimes make the people being helped feel bad. They sometimes blame themselves for causing helpers trouble, and they can become all too aware of their powerless state.

An interesting footnote to all this: because Americans and other Western cultures love their independence, there is often a stigma to seeking help. It can be interpreted as reflecting dependency, a kind of weakness—which is why so many people have trouble asking for it.

It is fascinating what goes on in the minds of both people who need help and those who come to their rescue.

But all psychological explanations aside, it is always incredibly heartwarming to see strangers step in simply because a little voice tells them it's the right thing to do.

Whatever the motive, it never gets old.

YOU GOTTA LEARN TO SPEAK UP

Cʒ ᬯ

I have never understood why so much discrimination and racism is based on skin color. Why are we obsessed with pointing out the simple differences that are easy to see rather than appreciating our deeper, inner beauty?

When I was a kid growing up back in the 1960s and 1970s, my hometown of San Antonio, like much of America, was segregated. Mexican Americans lived on the west side of town, African Americans on the east side, and the white community on the north side. And never did the three sides mingle. However, my father and I would trim trees and cut the lawns on the north side of town.

We would also trek up there once a year on Halloween night. Kids from throughout the barrio would pile into our old pickup truck and we'd go trick-or-treating all over those manicured neighborhoods, where the treats were so much better.

But interracial relationships? Taboo. You almost never saw a Latino boy dating a white girl. In fact, it wasn't unusual to hear about a Mexican kid being beaten up for simply daring to take a blond, blue-eyed girl on a date. When it came to dating, everyone was expected to stick to "their own kind." The result was that too often we wound up becoming friends with, dating, and marrying only people within our own tribes.

At Denny Moe's Barbershop in Harlem, New York, our black actor Gabriel walks in for a haircut, followed by his white girlfriend, Kristin. Rachael, our black actor playing the hairdresser, reacts in shock to the white girlfriend. "What? You're dating a white girl? You couldn't find a strong black woman for you?"

Reactions were immediate and strong. Denise Muldrow, an African American woman waiting for a haircut, just had to say something. "You are a real hater," she said to our hairdresser. "You're ignorant and insecure. Keep your opinions to yourself, because you sound stupid."

Why did Denise react so strongly? "You know, you gotta learn to speak up, especially when something's wrong," she told me. "Don't sit around anywhere where you're not feeling comfortable. Speak up."

Sitting next to her was Nicholas Richards, a local preacher. Between his shave and haircut, he put everything into perspective: "Hate doesn't do anything but beget more hate."

We all felt like we'd gone to Sunday services—inspired by a little gospel at a barbershop in Harlem.

ACCEPT PEOPLE FOR WHO THEY ARE

CR ℘

I know firsthand what it's like to be ridiculed because you don't speak English or because you talk with a funny accent.

For some reason, if it's a Spanish accent, people often presume that you're not very smart. But if it's a British, Australian, or French accent, it's perceived as somehow classier, more sophisticated. They are all accents, just the same!

I don't get it.

My parents took great pride in their Mexican roots. They were also proud Americans. They taught me and my sisters to appreciate the best of both worlds. But, in San Antonio, where the population is more than fifty percent Hispanic, folks could easily get by without speaking English, especially in the barrio where everyone was Latino. Catholic mass at St. Timothy's Church was in Spanish, business at local stores was conducted in Spanish. Even the radio stations we listened to and the TV channel we watched – Univision – was in Spanish. It certainly wasn't easy.

And yet, Bruno and Maria realized that, for their children to succeed in America, we would all have to master.

I'll never forget my first day in public school in San Antonio.

First grade at Carvajal Elementary, Mrs. Gregory's class. I spoke no English; my teacher spoke no Spanish.

I was sitting there, rather dumbfounded, with no idea what Mrs. Gregory was saying, when suddenly the school bell rang. It was ten a.m., recess time, and all the kids rushed outside to the playground.

Where did little Juanito Quiñones go? I walked home. I lived just a block from the school, and when I got home, my sweet mother, Maria, was obviously surprised. "*¿Que pasó, Juanito?* What happened?" she asked.

"*Se acabó.* It's over. I *like* school, Mom. Just two hours and, boom, we're done. I think this is going to work out nicely!" I responded in Spanish.

She grabbed me by the ear and walked me back to class. Eventually, I mastered the English language, but it took years to do it.

In a restaurant in Springfield, Missouri, a Latino mother and daughter were having lunch. The little girl spoke fluent English, but her mom did not and was struggling with the menu. A few tables away, Jeremy, our bigoted character, started lashing out at them.

"Hey, why don't you speak *English*?" he yelled. "This is America. We speak English!"

Several other diners clearly heard the insults but refused to get involved. They sat uncomfortably and just looked the other way.

"You don't look American," our bigot continued. "Foreigners are ruining the whole country!"

Suddenly, Paul Breckner, who was sitting with his family a few tables away, spoke up. "What exactly does 'American' look like? Let's face it—unless you're Native American, you're an immigrant, too."

And then the Breckner family did something totally unexpected. They invited our Hispanic mother and daughter to sit and have lunch with them.

"America is the melting pot of the world," Mrs. Breckner told me as the two families broke bread together. "We have to accept people for who they are . . . wherever they came from."

The response from this beautiful family was so heartwarming that even our actors were misty-eyed.

As for speaking English, of course it's important for any new immigrant to learn and master the language. But as they struggle toward that end, instead of ridiculing them, we should applaud them.

Besides, how boring would this country be if we all looked and sounded the same?

GEOGRAPHY MATTERS

❦

We live in an era when the world is now, literally, at our fingertips. We want to get in touch with other cultures in other lands? All we have to do is tap the screens on our little smartphones and we're there.

In that sense, we are better educated and certainly more aware of what's going on in places beyond our own communities. Even if you live in an area where there is not much ethnic diversity, or where people's religions or sexual orientations are all basically the same, you can explore other lifestyles on the Web, right in your living room.

But does that mean we are all now more accepting—more tolerant —of lifestyles and cultures that are different from our own? Not exactly.

We film many of our *WWYD* scenarios around the New York City area, the great American melting pot. More than eight hundred languages are spoken in New York, making it the most linguistically diverse city in the world.

On any given day, I will interact with people from India, Mexico, Russia and the Philippines.

In places like New York City, diversity reigns supreme. We are surrounded by people of different colors, creeds, and religions, and therefore we almost *have* to get along with each other. Otherwise, we wouldn't be able to carry on with our day.

In more monolithic areas of the country, there is less diversity and, as a result, sometimes less understanding of those of different races and cultures. When you live in a place where you've never met a black person, or a Latino, or a Jewish person, or a Muslim, you may have a tendency to make assumptions about them. And often those generalities can be wrong.

That's why every couple of months we pack up our *WWYD* cameras and take the show on the road. At times, the results—even in this day and age—have been startling.

Like the day we set up our hidden cameras in a diner in Brigham City, Utah—where the closest African American lives more than an hour away. The scenario: a white man berated his college-age daughter simply because she was dating a black man.

As usual in most of our shoots, many people refused to get involved. But several other diners spoke up in defense of our inter-racial couple.

And then along came two elderly white ladies, who suddenly broke down in tears when they saw our father acting upset over his daughter's black boyfriend.

"We feel for you," one of the ladies told our dad. "You have such a beautiful daughter and she's with *that?*"

Behind the scenes, I shook my head in disbelief, almost afraid to go out and interview the two women. But when I did, they simply continued with their racist tirade.

Toward the end of our interview, one of the women took my hand and said, "Now, Mexicans, you're all right. I would gladly marry you!"

After the piece aired, I got dozens of e-mails and tweets from viewers telling me, "Don't do it, John!"

After many years of filming *WWYD*, we have found that racial biases exist everywhere. But they are generally less prevalent in bigger cities where populations are more diverse. The reason is very simple: if you have the opportunity—and make the effort—to get to know someone of a different ethnicity on a personal level, you're less likely to buy into the generalities and stereotypes about that person's race.

Whenever I meet people whose backgrounds are different from mine, I make it a point to give them a big smile and start a conversation. I ask questions about their lives, their families, and their homelands.

It's harder to dislike people or make negative assumptions about their cultures or ethnicities once you get to know them.

More often than not, I've discovered that our aspirations, love of family, and pursuit of happiness are very much alike—no matter where we come from.

Underneath those outside appearances, our similarities often outweigh our differences.

EMBRACE OUR DIFFERENCES

☙ ❧

Because we've been monitoring human behavior for so long on *WWYD*, people often ask me, "Are you inspired or disappointed by how people react to different situations? Has your faith in humanity been lost or restored?"

As a "glass half full" kind of guy, I always choose to point to and applaud those everyday heroes who respond to someone who pretends to be in trouble. Of course, there are people who don't get involved or refuse to help. They remain quiet and detached for any number of reasons.

They may stand back because they're terribly shy or they're worried about getting sued in our very litigious society. Or they're afraid of becoming targets themselves. We need to give them the benefit of the doubt.

But that makes those people who *do* step in—sometimes at great risk to themselves—all the more impressive. Many times they do it with such wonderful candor and empathy that it overshadows everything else. All the members of our *WWYD* team—as well as our millions of viewers—walk away inspired, our faith in society, indeed, restored.

It is especially impressive when our scenarios involve race, bias, and discrimination. Those who speak up in defense of someone of a different ethnicity or religion are an eloquent reminder that we should never be defined by the color of our skin or the particular God we worship.

Yet there's no denying that racism still exists in this country—which prompts the question, are we, as human beings, inherently racist?

No, say the experts. People are not destined to behave in a racist way. Some do, but most do not. But whether we recognize it or not, we do tend to be *biased* against other types of people. Aspects of our psychology make it easy to learn to see others as representative of types rather than as individuals who are more similar than different from us.

We have seen bias a lot in reaction to our staged scenarios. For example, when teenage boys are discovered sleeping in a car, passersby are more likely to call 911 if the kids are black rather than white. If teens skip out on a restaurant tab, again patrons are more likely to call the police if the "dining dashers" are black.

People don't necessarily *know* they are being biased; it is just that they *percieve* the situation as more dangerous when the kids are black.

The experts we talk to are not surprised by that. Social psychology researchers have shown that many people automatically connect the color black and black faces with thoughts of aggression, threat, and crime without realizing it. Growing up in environments where bias is all around us creates more of the same. These automatic associations are learned so well they are hard to control. It takes mental effort to go against our own tide and rethink what we've learned to feel about people of different races and groups.

Blacks, Latinos, and Asians also have their own preconceived notions about each other—and about whites. In other words, we all do it.

You have to share the outrage of the victim and empathize with that person as a *fellow human being*. The key is to see everyone, regardless of race, as an individual, a person with needs and desires like any other human being.

Once we find that kinship and empathize with each other, we're on our way toward overcoming racism in this country . . . and everywhere else on the planet.

WHERE IS YOUR CARING HEART?

Cʒ ᏸↄ

People in different parts of the country also react in starkly contrasting ways when it comes to gay and broader LGBT issues.

When I was a kid growing up in south Texas, I didn't know anyone who was homosexual. Let me explain. There were certainly young people I knew who were gay. They just didn't tell anyone, because homosexuality was taboo back then. It was the 1960s, and even though gays were making great progress toward acceptance in other parts of the country, that was not the case in the strong Catholic enclave of San Antonio. To make matters worse, I lived in a very closed-minded—and, yes, macho—Latino community.

When I finally met my first openly gay fellow student in college, I realized the ugly ridicule and injustice he, and so many others, were suffering. I was angry and ashamed by the way my church and community condemned them. I just didn't get it. How is masculinity threatened by someone else's homosexuality? How can any religion condemn people for professing love toward each other?

Today in major American cities homosexuality is hardly an issue. But in certain, smaller pockets of the country, too much of that antigay mentality that I witnessed in Texas still exists.

On another one of our *WWYD* road trips, we traveled to the old Civil War town of Vicksburg, Mississippi. How would the residents in this very conservative part of America react to a gay couple showing affection toward each other?

While on a lunch date, our two actors held hands, hugged, and kissed. It was nothing outrageous, just pretty much what a heterosexual couple might do when expressing their love.

We then had an antagonist, another actor, complain about our couple. Almost immediately, people in the restaurant started weighing in, agreeing with her. And unlike what we heard when we staged the same scenario in larger cities, religion almost always fueled reactions in this small town.

"It's in the Bible. I believe in the Bible, and I love my Jesus."

"God's intention is one man, one woman. It's Adam and Eve . . . *not* Adam and Steve!"

"It goes against everything—against God. He said it's an abomination. Gays are not going to Heaven."

We were about ready to wrap up for the day when two young college students walked into the restaurant. As they heard the ugly comments about our gay couple, they started physically shaking in anger.

"This is the reason half the f--king world hates America," one of them said. "It's because of people like you. Because you have no acceptance for anything else in the world."

Those young men were twenty-two years old.

Clearly, thanks in large part to that younger generation, America has come a long way since those intolerant days in south Texas a few decades ago. More and more states now legally allow same-sex marriages. Today 60 percent of Americans say gays should have the same rights and privileges as the straight population.

But then there's that remaining 40 percent who disagree—pockets of ignorance and intolerance that should prompt all of us to ask, "Where is your caring heart?"

AGAINST ALL ODDS

Cʒ 𝔈ꝺ

There are times in life when you have to throw caution to the wind and go for it, because your assignment—your mission—is that important.

As a news correspondent, I've done that time and again, in places like Haiti, Cuba, Panama, Iraq, and even Sierra Leone, Africa. I took risks—some might say unadvisedly so—because the story was incredibly important and, I felt, vital to our viewers.

There's something to be said for having that kind of dedication to your work. It doesn't matter whether you're harvesting tomatoes, designing a building, or reporting a television news story. When one door slams in your face, you have to look for another one.

In 1989, I was asked to fly with a camera crew to Panama City, Panama, because political tensions were escalating between the United States and that country's dictator, General Manuel Noriega. President George H. W. Bush had accused the general of being the middleman in the massive smuggling operation of cocaine from Colombia, through Panama, to the United States.

There was only one problem with our assignment: neither I nor my crew had visas to enter Panama. General Noriega had stopped issuing them to journalists.

It had already been a hectic and dangerous December for us. For days I, along with my ABC producer Robert Campos and cameraman Joe LoMonaco, had been pinned down under gunfire in El Salvador while covering the civil war there.

After that, we traveled to Bogotá, Colombia, to cover the capture and killing of Gonzalo Rodriguez Gacha, one of that country's leading narco-traffickers.

So by the time we got the call to head to Panama, we were flying high on adrenaline. It didn't matter that we had no visas to enter the country. We were sure we could talk our way in.

First we flew from Bogotá to Panama City on a private charter jet—only to have soldiers board our plane on arrival and order the jet back to Colombia.

When I called ABC News in New York to tell them the bad news, I could hear the distress on the other end of the line from our foreign assignment desk chief.

There were now rumors that the United States was about to launch a military assault on Panama to capture General Noriega. All our competition—NBC News, CBS News, and CNN—already had their correspondents inside Panama. They had applied for and received their visas weeks before. ABC was the only network with no reporter on the ground.

We were desperate. We simply had to get ourselves inside Panama. That night, we decided to try again, flying into Panama on a commercial jet. Once again, when we landed—with no visas—we were denied entry. And this time an armed guard was assigned to watch over us while we waited for the next plane back to Colombia.

After several hours, our guard got tired and left, convinced that we wouldn't be able to get past the immigration counter without our visas.

I saw an opportunity. An Eastern Air Lines flight arrived from Miami, and its load of passengers started heading for the immigration counter.

"Why don't we get in line with them?" I said to my producer. "We can just pretend we're with that crowd and then tell the officials we've lost our visas."

Robert, of course, also wanted to get into Panama, but he worried that if we were caught sneaking in, we would be banned from ever entering the country.

He finally agreed with my plan. But by the time we got to the immigration desk, the planeload of passengers from Miami had already gone through, and the immigration agent had disappeared into a back room.

"Let's just keep walking," I whispered to Robert. Suddenly, the agent was back, yelling at us as we headed toward baggage claim.

"Hey," he shouted in Spanish. "Are you guys Panamanian?"

We just nodded. Panamanians, of course, don't need visas when they return to their own country.

Just like that, we were in, thanks to our ingenuity and one tired immigration agent. Of course, it didn't hurt that Robert and I are both Latino, speak Spanish, and can pass for Panamanians.

I will never forget the words from our assignment manager when we called ABC News that night from our hotel room in Panama City.

"John," he said, "if there were ever two men I would kiss on the lips, right now . . . it would be the two of you!"

The next day I was on the air live from Panama on *Good Morning America*.

All because we wouldn't take no for an answer and kept pushing. Against all the odds.

BEST-LAID PLANS

Cʒ ৪০

We had done it! Our persistence paid off, and my producer and I had successfully snuck into Panama. And there I was, reporting live about the imminent invasion by U.S. military forces. I was very proud of myself, and in New York, everyone at ABC News was breathing a sigh of relief.

But sometimes just when you think you've pulled one over on the universe, it comes back to bite you.

I had no idea that within twenty-four hours, Robert Campos, my ABC News producer, would be kidnapped by the Panamanian military.

Talk about guilt. Robert was like a brother to me. He would never have been taken hostage if I had not pressured him into joining me as I talked our way through the Panama City airport.

There he was, held at gunpoint by trigger-happy kidnappers in the basement of some undisclosed building downtown. Talk about a *What Would You Do?* dilemma.

It had all begun the night before as the United States launched

"Operation Just Cause." Robert and I had checked into the Marriott hotel in the capital, Panama City.

Around midnight, American forces began bombing the airport and the military headquarters of the dictator General Manuel Noriega. I had a very strong suspicion that in retaliation, Noriega's forces would attack our hotel, because that's where some one hundred American journalists were staying.

I was right. As Robert and I were meeting in my room, discussing how we would report the story, armed gunmen suddenly stormed the hotel lobby. Peeking through our window, we could see Panamanian soldiers marching forty of our colleagues out the front door.

For what seemed like hours, we could hear the cries and screams of other journalists as they were taken from adjoining rooms.

Then came the pounding on my door. Robert and I hit the floor and stayed there, motionless, next to my bed. The banging and the soldiers' yelling got louder and louder until, finally, they moved on. Fortunately, they didn't try to shoot their way in.

My throat was so parched from fear I couldn't whisper a single word.

Lying there, petrified, I quietly turned on a small transistor radio. We listened to the ABC News coverage of the invasion, which was being aired on the U.S. Armed Forces Radio Network. It was surreal. We could hear Peter Jennings reporting that forty American journalists had been taken hostage from the hotel. Live on the air, Peter announced that ABC suspected Robert and I were among those kidnapped!

You can imagine how my poor elderly mother and Robert's young wife felt as they watched that news back in the States. But there was no way for us to call them—or ABC News—because all phone calls from the hotel were being monitored by the dictator's forces.

Finally, around five in the morning, our cameraman knocked on the hotel room door. I could see through the peephole that he was in tears.

"They took so many reporters," he said. "But it's okay now, the soldiers are gone."

Our relief was short-lived. Later that day, while I was on the air, Noriega's armed thugs once again stormed the hotel lobby. They grabbed even more American journalists. And this time they took Robert Campos.

At gunpoint, they forced him and a CBS producer into the back of a pickup. With a rifle jammed into the back of his knees, he was driven through bumpy streets to a hidden basement, where the thugs threatened to kill him and the other producer.

On the air with Peter Jennings that day, I kept complaining about how Panama's military had kidnapped so many innocent journalists—including our own producer.

During a commercial break, Peter asked me to stop talking about it. He pointed out that it sounded self-serving. In the midst of this invasion, there were many more American soldiers whose lives were also at risk.

As a reporter, I knew Peter was right. But as a human being, I was worried about my good friend and colleague.

As luck would have it, among the people taken hostage with Robert that morning was Daniel Sarria, the general manager of the Marriott, who was taken because he wouldn't give the soldiers the room numbers of the American journalists staying at the hotel. Daniel was an incredibly principled—and brave—man.

And he was the man who may well have saved Robert's life. The two were separated from the other captives, and as they stood back to back with their hands tied, they were told they would pay for what President Bush was doing to Panama.

Daniel told his captors that he knew "important people" in Panama. The guards didn't believe him, but to appease him, they dialed a number he gave them. A woman on the other end answered and proceeded to read the guards the riot act.

It was Daniel's wife, who was very well known in Panama. Even more important, her sister was General Noriega's mistress!

The soldiers quickly untied him and told him he was free to go. Instead of running for his life, Daniel boldly announced, "Mr. Campos is a guest of my hotel and I cannot leave without him."

Begrudgingly, one of the captors then also untied Robert, but not before staring inches from his face and warning him, "Don't you dare talk to the press."

Late that night, I was getting ready to leave the hotel, along with the other remaining journalists. It was simply getting too dangerous for us to remain there.

Suddenly, out of nowhere, Robert staggered into the lobby, looking as though he had just walked through Hell.

Through tears, we held on to each other for the longest time before we were whisked away to the safety of a foreign ambassador's house.

And finally, Robert managed to crack the smile of a man who had just been given a new lease on life.

SHINING THE LIGHT OF JOURNALISM

CȢ Ȣ

Imagine you're sitting in a pitch-black room and you cannot even see your hand in front of your face. The journalist is the one person with a candle, shining light on the darkest corners of the room. They can illuminate injustice, corruption, human rights violations. That's how I define journalism.

Shining the light, giving a voice to people who have none. When we, as reporters, get it right—and we often don't—that is the work we should be doing.

In 1991, that was precisely what drove me to Haiti and the Dominican Republic on an investigative story for the ABC news-magazine *Primetime Live*.

I had heard that Haitian children—as young as seven and eight years old—were being kidnapped on that country's border with the Dominican Republic and then forced to work as virtual slaves harvesting sugarcane at government-owned plantations.

We flew into Port-au-Prince, Haiti, where we met up with a smuggler who recruited children—under the false promise of good money—and then transported them to the sugarcane fields of the Dominican Republic. There, the kids would work every day from dawn till dusk, earning the equivalent of about three dollars a day, barely enough money to feed themselves.

The cane they harvested was refined and then sold to American sugar companies.

Before our story aired on ABC News, Americans had no idea that much of the sugar in their coffee, soft drinks, and virtually every other food product they consumed was being harvested by children under slave-like conditions.

I will never forget the face of little Horacio Liveli, a ten-year-old Haitian boy we met on one of the sugarcane plantations near the town of La Romana. Through tears, he told us he was sold into slavery by Dominican smugglers for just twelve dollars.

"I have nothing to eat," he told me. "I cry every day because we suffer so much misery. We are slaves who work for almost nothing."

His hands—like the hands of many of these young workers— were covered with cuts and bruises from the machetes they used to cut the huge stalks of cane. Older workers had gouged eyes and severed fingers, the scars of the cane fields.

Hundreds of children, like Horacio, were kept on the plantations at gunpoint, watched over by armed guards on horseback. "They treat us like animals," another boy told me.

Every night when we got back to our hotel, my producer Robert Campos, cameraman Joe LoMonaco, and soundman Steve Blanco— tough guys who had witnessed all kinds of tragedy—were almost in tears, heartbroken by what we saw in those cane fields.

When we asked Dominican government officials about the plight of these children, the woman who oversaw the plantations admitted their working conditions were "depressed," but added, "They're not much worse than what these workers left behind in Haiti."

It's at times like these that I have felt like ripping off my reporter's hat, yelling at the authorities, and rescuing those innocent victims myself.

But the beautiful thing about journalism is that often while nosing around, exposing injustice, we're able to find good people who are willing to right the wrongs.

While filming in the sugarcane fields of the Dominican Republic, we met Father Edwin Paraison, an Episcopal priest from Haiti who had created a foundation to locate the slave children and return them to their homeland.

"These are children who should be holding notebooks and pencils in their hands," he told us. "Instead, they're holding machetes. It is despicable."

We were on one of the plantations filming the kids at work when Father Paraison arrived, loaded the underage workers into the back of his pickup truck, and drove them three hundred miles back to their families in Haiti.

As the children disappeared down the dusty road leading out of the cane fields, the Haitian workers left behind broke into song. "Good-bye, my brothers, good-bye," they sang. "If we don't see you in our homeland, we will see you in Heaven."

The day after my report aired on *Primetime Live*, in Washington, an ambassador from the Dominican Republic held a news conference accusing me and ABC News of fabricating the whole story. He claimed we used actors to pose as Haitian sugarcane cutters.

But the ambassador had no explanation for what happened in the Dominican Republic over the following several weeks. Father Paraison continued making trips to the cane fields, rescuing and relocating several hundred more Haitian children. There was no getting around it: these were no actors; they were slaves.

I was never more proud of our investigative light than when we shined it on those sugarcane fields of the Dominican Republic.

BE BOLD. BE SMART. THEN GO FOR IT.

Cʒ ঠৎ

Miracles start to happen when you give as much energy to your dreams as you do to your fears.

Yet often fear—usually fear of the unknown—holds us back. We simply give it too much energy. We don't apply for that plum job because we don't think we're good enough. We don't approach someone we're attracted to because we're afraid we'll be turned down. We don't raise a hand to ask a simple question because we think we'll be laughed at. We don't take the road less traveled because of some phantom evil that might lurk around the corner.

As a result, we stick to the comfort and the safety of routine, never realizing what could have been if we had only taken that chance.

We've all heard the saying "the greater the risk, the greater the reward." It doesn't always have to be all about money or fame. For a teacher, the reward from educating kids at a crime-ridden inner-city school is making a difference in a young person's life. For a lawyer working pro bono cases, the payoff is proving the innocence of someone who has been wrongfully accused or convicted. For doctors and nurses working in impoverished neighborhoods, the reward is providing medical care that might well save a patient's life.

In journalism, the greatest reward comes from exposing wrong-doing, correcting injustice, and shining the light on corruption and human rights violations.

Unfortunately, those stories almost always come with the greatest risk.

In the late 1990s, I traveled to the West African nation of Sierra Leone for a story on blood diamonds. The country was incredibly rich in the precious stones, but precisely because of that, it had also become one of the most dangerous places on the planet.

A brutal rebel group known as the Revolutionary United Front (RUF) had overtaken Sierra Leone's government and the country's diamond-mining fields. After forcing slaves to mine the gems, the rebels would sell the diamonds on the black market. They would then use the millions of dollars in profit to buy weapons to wage their insurgency.

People from all over the world—including the United States—had no idea that the money they paid for their beautiful and expensive diamonds was being used to wage a bloody civil war in this far-off land.

It was atrocious. The RUF abducted boys and girls—some as young as five years old—to serve as child soldiers and prostitutes, often forcing them to murder their own parents.

The rebels were known to carve the initials RUF into their chests. Officers would then rub cocaine into the open wounds to make the soldiers maniacal and fearless.

The atrocities got worse and worse. Brandishing their trademark machetes, the rebels would cut off the hands, arms, and legs of anyone who might disagree with them, including tens of thousands of innocent civilians. Among the victims were infants and children.

Obviously, this was a huge story that needed to be exposed, but with it came serious danger. Already, fifteen journalists had been killed covering the story.

As I discussed the assignment with my producers at ABC News, we weighed all the risks and then decided I would travel to Sierra Leone with a producer and a camera crew. We would limit our time on the ground to only five days.

Some of the reporters killed had been attacked at roadblocks set up by the rebels, so we agreed that we would travel only by helicopter.

We would also be accompanied by a team of armed South African security guards. Never in my life had I been so well protected.

Were we nervous flying into Sierra Leone? Of course, but we never lost sight of the greater good that would come from broadcasting the story.

Our first stop: a refugee center in the capital, Freetown, where we met hundreds of Sierra Leoneans living in squalor, all of them amputees. Men, women, and children—too many children—with severed arms, legs, fingers, and hands. The trademark punishment of those RUF rebels.

As I walked through the masses of people living in tents, I met one woman whose husband had been killed by the soldiers and whose sister had been raped. The ruthless rebels, high on cocaine, had then turned their machetes on her six-month-old baby, chopping off the infant's left arm.

In all my travels covering wars and natural disasters, I had never seen anything like it.

We then had to decide whether to venture toward RUF rebel territory, the diamond-mining fields farther away from the capital. Our producers in New York had told us they'd rather we didn't leave Freemont. But I knew it would be difficult to tell the story of blood diamonds without ever having seen how those precious stones were mined and by whom.

So after taking a vote among ourselves, my crew and I decided we would fly the helicopter—with those armed guards on board—on a very quick trip to the mining fields. The security team told our pilots to "hug the landscape" and fly just ten feet over the treetops of Sierra Leone's jungle. That way, the RUF might not see us coming and they would have a lesser chance of shooting us down.

Within twenty minutes, we landed in the diamond fields, where we met and interviewed several miners panning for the gems. They nervously explained that they were being forced to work under subhuman conditions by the RUF. We filmed them at work, shot my "stand-up," during which I talked about the mining, and then quickly made our exit. We accomplished all of that within fifteen minutes.

A few weeks later, when my story aired on *20/20*, it led to an international outcry. In July 2000, the World Diamond Congress instituted a ban on all blood diamonds that were mined in the so-called conflict zones, including Sierra Leone.

And then, on January 18, 2001, President Clinton issued an executive order that prohibited the importation of all rough diamonds from Sierra Leone to the United States.

The public was educated, laws were passed, and policies changed. Soon the RUF's vicious war was at an end.

Thousands of lives were saved because journalists—with a measured and calculated approach—chose to shine their light on war and atrocities.

You limit the risks, but you never let fear dominate.

TAKE ON A NEW CHALLENGE

C3 80

It is easy to get comfortable with our daily routines. We do the same kind of work day in and day out. We surround ourselves with the same kinds of people. We do the same things in our leisure time.

Familiarity keeps things simple. Pretty soon our routine becomes second nature. And we're presented with few surprises and risks. Routine is safe and never much of a threat. But all too often it seems as if every day is a replay of yesterday. We stop growing, learning, evolving.

That's why I love filming *What Would You Do?* Within a few minutes, we shake up people's lives. An innocent bystander is suddenly witnessing something unusual, often disturbing, and it forces them to decide either to step in or to step away.

We force a dilemma, a challenge, upon them. I can almost see the wheels turning inside their heads. They're torn, unsure of what to do. Then, suddenly, folks who usually stay to themselves, mind their own business, and never get involved are sounding an alarm.

We have jolted them out of their comfort zone.

Journalists live at the other end of the spectrum. Nothing is ever quite routine. As a news correspondent, I've had to endure those "jump starts" more times than I can count.

One of the greatest jolts of my career came in 1991, when I was flying to India for ABC News. I was working on a story about the selling of human organs.

Impoverished women in outlying provinces of the country were undergoing surgery to remove one of their kidneys. They weren't sick. Their kidneys were perfectly fine. They were selling the vital body organ for cash—to people outside India, people who *were* sick and needed a kidney transplant.

Now, most of us are born with two kidneys, and if necessary, we can survive with only one of them. Kidney transplants are extremely common.

These women in India were going under the knife for this incredibly invasive operation simply because they were desperately poor. When I asked why only the women opted for the surgery, I was told that the men in these poor villages needed to remain healthy and strong enough to work. They were paid twelve hundred dollars for each kidney, which allowed the women to buy themselves a little kiosk or food cart. With that small business, they could take care of their families for the rest of their lives.

In addition, the transactions helped save the lives of people who were critically ill with kidney disease in places like the United States, Europe, and Asia.

But the broader ethical dilemma was this: what would *you* do if you were that impoverished Indian woman whose only hope for saving her family was selling that organ?

What if you were the father or mother of a child who was dying from kidney disease and needed that lifesaving transplant?

American and other Western doctors were repulsed by the idea. But medical professionals in India argued that outsiders should not be so quick to judge. Tens of thousands of Indian women were doing what they felt they had to do to survive.

By the same token, when it came to organ "donations," was it right for rich people who were desperately sick to take advantage of people who were desperately poor?

It was a complicated story. I met and interviewed people on both sides of the debate and walked away with no clear-cut answer of what was right or wrong. However, believe it not, the kidney story was not what disrupted my journalistic routine that particular week. The big jolt happened as my plane circled over New Delhi, about to land in the capital. An hour before touchdown, I was asleep when a flight attendant gently nudged me.

"Mr. Quiñones, the control tower radioed our captain in the cockpit a while ago and asked us to make sure you are the first person allowed off the plane when we land. There has been some kind of emergency and you need to get off as soon as possible."

"What's happened?" I asked.

"I have no idea," she said. "That's all we've been told, so gather up your bags."

My heart started racing. Had something happened to my kids back home? Was there something wrong with my mom or dad in Texas?

When the doors of the plane opened, I was first one off and was immediately greeted by a very excited Indian man.

"My name is Sharma," he said. "Give me your passport and come with me, quickly."

"Don't I have to clear customs and immigration?" I asked.

"It's all taken care of."

"What about my bags?"

"We'll come back for them later."

Within three minutes we were out of the Delhi airport and sitting in Sharma's car.

Finally, I blurted out, "Who exactly are you and what the hell is going on?"

"I run the ABC News office here in India. My name is Sharma," he repeated before dropping the bombshell. "Rajiv Gandhi, the former prime minister of India, has just been assassinated! And you're on the air, live on *Nightline*, in forty-five minutes!"

Just hours before, in southern India, Rajiv Gandhi had been killed by a suicide bomber while campaigning for congress. He was the son of Indira Gandhi, who, as prime minister of India, had also been assassinated, years before.

I was stunned and a nervous wreck. I had researched and prepared intensely for a story about kidney transplants but knew very little about Indian politics.

Now, in less than an hour, I had to appear live on television and explain to Ted Koppel the ramifications of this horrible tragedy in the midst of the world's largest democratic elections.

This is when you either crumble under the pressure or accept the challenge and go for it.

It is also the time when you rely on great support. Janice Tobias, my ABC producer from New York, had arrived in India a couple of days before me to prepare for the kidney story shoot. And she was all over the story of the assassination.

She quickly briefed me with the latest details on the killing and gave me a crash course in Indian politics.

I memorized as much information as I could, took a deep breath, and, as the red light on the camera turned on, went for it. I explained all I could to Mr. Koppel, who, fortunately, didn't grill me for too many more details.

Back in the States, ABC News was the first network on the air with a correspondent reporting on the assassination live from India. Our competition was left scratching their heads: "How in the world did John Quiñones get to India that fast?"

Little did they know it was just a bit of serendipity—and the strength to stare down fear and intimidation.

Don't limit your challenges. Challenge your limits.

WOULD YOU RISK YOUR LIFE FOR FREEDOM?

CB BD

My ultimate WWYD moment as a reporter came when I was filming a story in the middle of the Straits of Florida. It was a report about the plight of "Cuban rafters," immigrants who were so desperate to flee their communist island—and the tyranny of Fidel Castro—they floated to sea on whatever raft they could build. Their destination: the shores of Florida and the freedom of America—ninety miles away.

My camera crew and I actually started shooting our story in the air, flying over the Caribbean with a group of pilots from Miami who called themselves Brothers to the Rescue. They were Cuban American exiles on a humanitarian mission: scouring the sea for rafters. If they spotted any, they would alert the U.S. Coast Guard, which would send their vessels to rescue them.

Many of the rafters never made it.

José Basulto, the founder of Brothers to the Rescue, flew us to a deserted island somewhere near the Bahamas that was littered with the remnants of the makeshift boats: splintered wood, tires, and inner tubes. The Cuban men, women, and children who had bravely boarded those rickety rafts were lost at sea.

We decided to head toward Cuba on a charter boat ourselves, to get a closer look. About four hours after we set sail from Key West, Florida, we noticed a tiny blip on the horizon. Slowly, it came into focus. A raft made of flimsy balsa wood, loaded with a family of six Cuban refugees.

We quickly realized why they were frantically waving and screaming at us. Their float, no bigger than eight feet square, was sinking. We urgently called the coast guard. The response: their closest ship was too far away and could never make it in time to save them.

And then, a request: "Can you guys rescue the rafters yourselves?"

As journalists, we're supposed to report the news, not *make* it. We generally try to keep our distance and not alter the story with our involvement.

But this was different. People's lives were in peril. It was a no-brainer.

We had to do whatever we could to rescue this family. We immediately sped toward the small sinking vessel and pulled its occupants onto our boat: an elderly couple, their middle-aged son and his wife, and their two small children.

Three generations of Cuban immigrants who had given up everything they owned, leaving the rest of their family behind on the island, for this one shot at starting new lives in the United States.

The patriarch of the family, seventy-eight-year-old Rafael

Castillo, a small, barefoot, frail man in a tattered T-shirt and shorts, fell into my arms, sobbing with appreciation. He told me they had run out of food and water and were hallucinating from hunger and dehydration. They thought they would all surely perish at sea.

We gave them water and food and then ferried them to Key West, where the Castillo family was processed by U.S. immigration officials. Because the government determined the family—like so many other Cubans—was fleeing political persecution, they were allowed to remain in the United States.

How many other Cubans were just as desperate to leave the island? We decided to fly to Havana to find out. I had heard that every week hundreds of people were making the same treacherous journey across the Straits of Florida from the small port city of Cojimar, just thirty miles from the capital.

The Cuban government, of course, didn't want foreign journalists to write or broadcast the story. So my cameraman, Jerry Gonzalez, and I went undercover to investigate.

What we found was astounding. Under the cover of darkness, the town of Cojimar had been converted into a boat-building mecca. In virtually every backyard, people—mostly young men—were busy hammering and sawing any piece of wood they could find. The preferred choice was balsa, a very lightweight wood that floats easily on the water. That's why the Cuban boat people were called *balseros*.

They would tie the lumber or tree limbs to old tires, empty plastic jugs, inner tubes—anything that might keep their rafts from sinking.

At dawn the next day, a huge crowd gathered on Cojimar's

shores as the men carried dozens of makeshift boats on their shoulders and then dropped them into the water.

It was a massive, tearful farewell. Mothers, wives, and daughters kissing sons, husbands, and fathers as they piled onto their little rafts and floated away, none of them really knowing if they'd ever see each other again.

I had never witnessed anything like it.

The next time you catch yourself complaining about your condition in life, and how bad things are in your country—whatever that might be—think about those *balseros*, the boat people of Cuba.

Things might not be so bad after all.

WHAT WOULD YOU DO TO BE FREE?

C8 80

Sometimes I wish I could wave a magic wand so that every American could realize and appreciate all the freedoms this great country has afforded us. Obviously, we still have our share of problems, but compared to other nations, we enjoy some amazing rights and privileges. Among them, of course, are the freedoms of speech, religion, and the press and the right to bear arms. No wonder so many people from all over the world are willing to do whatever it takes to get here.

How far would you be willing to go to acquire freedom? What if your children were in peril? Would you risk your life—and theirs—on a dangerous journey to a land of opportunity?

Illegal immigration continues to be one of our most pressing hot-button political issues. I've done dozens of stories on it, including a report for a local TV station in Chicago that earned me my first Emmy Award.

As a reporter for WBBM in Chicago, I went undercover on the U.S.-Mexico border, posing as a Mexican immigrant trying to get into the United States. Actually, I first traveled to a small impoverished town in Mexico composed mostly of women and children. Virtually all the men had journeyed, illegally, to the United States to find work and send money back to their families. It was a desperate bid for the freedom—that all-too-human right—for survival. I like to think that immigrants are like victims in an abusive relationship. Don't they have a basic right to leave that awful existence to protect their families?

In the border town of Nuevo Laredo, Mexico, I spoke only Spanish and pretended to be just another immigrant looking for a smuggler—a "coyote"—to ferry me across the Rio Grande to Laredo, Texas. Sure enough, within a couple of hours I found one. "Julio" and I met at a church courtyard, where for three hundred dollars he sold me a fake birth certificate and social security card, all captured on hidden camera.

That night, we met on the bank of the river, where Julio instructed me to strip down to my underwear and put my clothes in a plastic bag. Talk about feeling vulnerable. Smugglers often rob, assault, and kill would-be immigrants, then toss their bodies into the Rio Grande.

Luckily, I had found a somewhat more benevolent coyote. As the sun set on the border, I slipped onto an inner tube and Julio pushed me through the river's murky waters toward the U.S. side of the border—where my camera crew was hiding in the bushes, recording it all.

After my trek across the border, I went back to Chicago, where, still undercover, I got a job as a dishwasher at a Greek restaurant.

A RETURN TO THE BORDER

CR 80

It is amazing to me how—for so many decades—immigration has remained such a controversial issue. Twenty-five years after I floated across the Rio Grande for that story on undocumented workers, I returned to the border for ABC News. This time, producer Bert Rudman, cameraman Jerry Gonzalez, and I journeyed to a region in southern Arizona aptly known as *El Camino del Diablo*—the Devil's Highway. Over the years, thousands of immigrants from Mexico and Central America have perished along this barren and dangerous stretch of the Sonoran Desert while trying to make it to the promised land.

Each of them paid anywhere from three to five thousand dollars to smugglers who vowed to guide them toward Tucson, Phoenix, and points beyond.

In recent years, the United States Immigration and Customs Enforcement agency had been beefing up its presence and building higher fences along the two-thousand-mile-long border between the two Americas. But because it is so desolate and its temperatures scorching hot, the Devil's Highway had fewer border-patrol agents on surveillance and, therefore, had become the entry point of choice for immigrants crossing illegally into the United States.

They often included women and children. They were told by the coyotes, that they would need only a couple of jugs of water for the trek. Tragically and mercilessly, they were never told the hike to Tucson was seventy miles long and it would take at least three days and three nights. No one mentioned that they could not physically carry enough food and water to survive. And because of that, many perished.

We felt there was no better way to tell the story of this treacherous journey than to experience it ourselves. So in the Mexican town of Nogales, which straddles the U.S.-Mexico border, my crew and I met up with four men who were about to embark on the desert crossing. They agreed to let us go along with them.

Our producer Bert would be following us in a van, driving north on a highway just a few miles away. He was carrying box loads of food and water bottles. Jerry and I were equipped with satellite phones. In case of any emergency, we would be able to summon help immediately. It was a luxury no other immigrants who cross the Devil's Highway ever have.

Our fellow travelers were a fifteen-year-old street kid from Guatemala, a thirty-year-old unemployed carpenter from El Salvador, and two peasants from Mexico: a man in his thirties and "Ricardo," a sixty-two-year-old grandfather. I have no idea how they saved up the money to pay their coyote.

The trek would be the longest, most arduous hike of my life. It was August, and by noon temperatures reached 130 degrees. We were drenched in sweat and already running out of water. As we walked through the desert, we spotted human bones, discarded shoes and clothing, empty water jugs, and even abandoned baby strollers. We could only wonder what happened to those poor, unfortunate infants and the guilt-ridden parents who made the awful mistake of bringing them along on their journey.

The Sonoran Desert is a minefield of saguaro and barrel cacti, and we were covered with their barbed needles. By nightfall, Jerry's hiking boots dissolved into shreds and all of us had run out of water. But then, miracle of all miracles: suddenly, on the horizon, there was what seemed like a mirage—four huge tanks of drinking water! It turned out church groups in the area had placed the tanks strategically in the desert as a humanitarian gesture. There were water stops every five hours along our path. The U.S. immigration service wasn't happy about it, but those church groups were literally saving lives.

We prepared to spend our first night in the desert, and I felt terribly guilty as I unfurled my sleeping bag and munched on PowerBars. I offered them to the rest of the group, but they politely declined, opting instead for their bean-and-tortilla tacos.

I couldn't but notice Ricardo, the old man in our group, carefully laying out his makeshift blanket—a serape—on the cold, hard ground. He then took a clove of garlic from his pocket and rubbed it on the ground, making a big circle in the sand. I was mystified.

"Why are you doing that?" I asked.

"It's for the snakes," he said. "They hate the smell of garlic. It keeps them away."

"Por favor," I said. "Please give me some of that." I slept much better that night and the next.

We spent forty-eight hours with our fellow travelers, and after walking thirty-five miles together, we parted ways. Bert, Jerry, and I emerged from the Sonoran Desert with some unique insight on the immigration story—and a much greater appreciation for the little things.

We immediately checked into a nice hotel in Tucson. And our four new amigos from Mexico and Central America? They just kept walking . . . in search of jobs and a better life.

LOVE YOUR LIFE

C3 80

My job as a general assignment reporter for *World News Tonight* was a dream come true.

But the more I watched ABC's newsmagazines, *Primetime Live* and *20/20*, the more I also wanted to work for them. Their stories were longer, more investigative and in-depth.

I kept bugging my bosses to let me report for those shows but was repeatedly turned down. "Thanks for your interest, John," they would tell me. "But we have our own special veteran correspondents for the newsmagazines."

Well, if you know anything about me, it is that I have never taken no for an answer.

I just kept looking for an opportunity to burst onto those shows with some great story.

My big break came when I was on assignment in Colombia, covering that country's presidential election. There was a great deal of interest in the story because of the ongoing violence of drug wars in South America.

But the election went off peacefully and I was asked by ABC to return to the States.

The night before we flew back from Bogotá, my crew and I were walking to our hotel from dinner when we noticed a group of homeless children. They were huddled on a dark street corner, getting high by sniffing glue.

When a police officer started questioning them, the kids ran to the middle of the street and did something that baffled us. Together, they lifted one of those heavy iron manhole covers on the pavement and then climbed down into the dark underground tunnel.

That was when it hit us: the children lived in the sewers of Bogotá.

When I asked our local Colombian contact who they were, she explained that the children were called *gamines*, Spanish for "street urchins." They were orphans, runaways, or kids who had simply been abandoned by their families. Regardless of how they had gotten there, some three hundred of them lived in the sewers.

I knew I had a story—and not just a two-minute report for the evening news. This was a much deeper piece for a broadcast like *Primetime Live*, the brand-new ABC newsmagazine show anchored by Diane Sawyer and Sam Donaldson.

I remember nervously calling the show's executive producer, Rick Kaplan, at home in New York. I half expected to be yelled at for disturbing his family time on a Sunday night. Instead, he simply said, "John, if you guys are crazy enough to want to go into the sewers of Colombia for a story, who am I to say no? Go for it."

We were ecstatic. An opportunity to report for *Primetime Live*!

As we started filming the story of the sewer children, we learned that they survived by stealing from tourists during the day.

Colombian police and the country's military were on a campaign to get rid of the street children, but they would not dare venture into the sewers. As you might imagine, the underground bowels of this city of ten million were a festering cesspool of filth and disease.

Instead, the cops' approach to "solving" the problem was even more horrific. At night, they would open up those manhole covers, pour gasoline down the tunnels, and light a match and throw it in. They wanted to scorch the children out of hiding.

Several of the kids had been killed by the authorities, others horrifically burned.

"Is there anyone trying to help these kids?" I asked a woman who worked for ABC News in Bogotá.

"Really only one man," she said. "His name is Jaime Jaramillo. The kids call him a wealthy Colombian engineer who takes food to the kids at night and is trying to build an orphanage for them—with very little luck."

We set up a meeting with Jaime, who, as you might imagine, was an incredibly compassionate and loving man. He showed us pictures of some of the kids he had pulled out of those tunnels. The skin on their faces, necks, and arms looked like melted wax—the scars from those fires set by Colombian authorities.

Jaime earned half a million dollars a year searching for oil in Latin America for American petroleum companies. But he told us he couldn't sleep at night knowing that children were living in such horrific conditions. So he did what he could—even if it only meant taking a loaf of bread and a bucket of fried chicken to the kids in the middle of the night.

The kids called him Papa Jaime. They trusted him and no one else. I knew if we were going to take our cameras into their dark world, we would have to be escorted by the kids' forty-five-year-old savior. Papa Jaime agreed to take us down.

My producer Robert Campos, cameraman Joe LoMonaco, soundman Steven Blanco, and I spent a week in the stench- and disease-ridden underbelly of Bogotá. Wearing rubber boots, suits, and masks, we waded through rivers of waste, which at times rose all the way to our chests.

We were embarrassed. Here we were covered from head to toe in protective gear, and the kids were dressed in rags and had to endure those despicable conditions every single night. In the middle of our interviews, I would look at Robert, Joe, and Steve, and they were all in tears, heartbroken by what we were hearing and seeing.

The saddest of all was our interview with a sixteen-year-old girl who had given birth to a baby just two months before.

Can you imagine starting life in the sewer?

People often ask me, "How in the world can you do your job as a reporter when you are faced with that kind of misery? Doesn't it affect you?"

Of course it does. There are times when I am in tears or have nightmares about what I have witnessed. But I just keep reminding myself that when I document and put those stories on television, a greater good might prevail. And it makes it all worthwhile.

Sure enough, after my story from Colombia aired on *Primetime*

Live in the States, American viewers were so touched they started a fund-raising campaign. Within a week, Jaime Jaramillo and his fledgling foundation, called Fundación Niños de los Andes—"Children of the Andes"—had received a million dollars in donations.

Jaime was able to build a sprawling orphanage for the kids in Bogotá and they were all—safely—pulled out of the sewers. And he didn't stop there. He made sure all those kids got an education and job training to pursue trades and careers. He not only fed them fish; he taught them how to fish.

So far Papa Jaime has rescued some 30,000 children from the streets and sewers of Colombia.

"I don't care if I help one child or one thousand children," he says. "What's important to me is that the little boy or girl is able to expand their conscience and find their internal light in such darkness."

In return, the sewer kids have left us with an important reminder: compared to those who live in poverty and misery in many other parts of the world, those of us in places like the United States live like royalty.

Put yourself in the shoes of those Colombian children sleeping and eating—barely surviving—right next to raging rivers of fetid waste, and you quickly realize we have very little to complain about.

JEALOUSY

C3 80

Most of us experience it at one time or another: jealousy, that complex emotion that triggers all kinds of feelings ranging from fear of abandonment to humiliation to rage.

Usually jealousy brings about anger and fear. Anger that someone else is moving in on someone very close to you, and the fear of losing that special person. At the root of it all is insecurity.

As I write this chapter, I'm sitting in a Houston courtroom, where a famous Texas cancer specialist is on trial for trying to kill her lover.

Dr. Ana Maria Gonzalez-Angulo was angry because the man she was having an affair with, another cancer doctor, George Blumenschein, had told her he was ending the relationship for another woman.

Dr. Gonzalez-Angulo invited Dr. Blumenschein over to her home for one final romantic interlude and then served him a special brew of coffee she said she had brought from her homeland of Colombia.

Little did her lover know Dr. Gonzalez-Angulo had laced the coffee with ethylene glycol, the active ingredient in antifreeze.

Dr. Blumenschein drank the coffee and almost died. His kidneys now function at only 40 percent, and his heart was also badly damaged.

At the end of a weeklong trial, Dr. Gonzalez-Angulo was convicted and sentenced to ten years in prison. The lives of two brilliant doctors were all but ruined, simply because of jealousy.

Nothing good ever comes of it, even the silliest of jealousies.

Let's say a man is at a restaurant with his significant other, enjoying a romantic dinner, just the two of them. Suddenly, his friendly waiter becomes a little *too* friendly. He starts making comments about how attractive the man's girlfriend or wife is. The waiter winks at her, brings her an extra glass of wine, touches her hair. He's even convinced they might have met before. Pretty soon, it's obvious he's hitting on her.

Meanwhile, he's totally ignoring the man . . . and being downright rude.

What would you do?

And what if it's a waitress flirting with a woman's boyfriend or husband?

It was one of the most memorable *WWYD* scenarios we've ever filmed. Of course, the person who was being flirted with was in on the act. But the partner had no idea. Despite however confident the partner was in the relationship, the green-eyed monster of jealousy appeared with nearly every unsolicited flirtation.

One husband got so upset he turned on his wife. "That waiter might be making you feel all giddy right now. But you're going home with me tonight and you'll have to deal with one angry husband."

Another woman erupted when the waitress touched her husband's hair, yelling, "You touch him again and I'm dumping this plate of food on your head!"

William Penn said it best: "the jealous are troublesome to others, but a torment to themselves." It can be so destructive and all-consuming.

Experts tell us jealousy is a signal that it's time for us to make a change in our lives that will allow us to move on to the next stage of our emotional growth.

The best reaction we got to our *WWYD* scenario was the response from a gay man whose partner was the object of flirtation from our waiter. He simply smiled and took it all as a compliment to the attractiveness of his mate.

"Look," he later told us, "you have to be confident in your relationship. I trust that my partner can handle this. If he's swayed by someone else's advances, then maybe our relationship was not meant to be. My being jealous and angry will only make things worse."

Instead, we should use our jealous reaction as a reason to work on ourselves . . . and identify and get rid of the fears that drive it.

TAKE THE HIGH ROAD

☙ ❧

We have all been hurt by the ugly comments or actions of people we once considered good friends . . . maybe even spouses, partners. We feel betrayed, insulted. We're left emotionally wounded and angry.

What would you do? What *should* you do?

The natural instinct is to strike back and get even by talking badly about them. Like children, we throw temper tantrums, trying to give the people who hurt us a bit of their own medicine. We go for the jugular.

Wrong move. I learned long ago that just because someone invites you to the drama doesn't mean you have to attend.

Fighting fire with fire might make us feel good temporarily, but in the long run, it only makes us look bad in the eyes of everyone else. You and your friend wind up arguing, trying to outdo each other with insults, which only damages the relationship further, perhaps permanently.

I heard a great quote the other day: "Weak people seek revenge.

Strong people forgive. Intelligent people ignore."

Be the strong and intelligent one. Reacting to someone at the same nasty level is easy, but it won't get you anywhere. Remain professional and respectable in your words and actions. Don't sink to the other person's level. Instead, be a person of integrity and class.

Remember that sometimes knowing when to *let go* of a disagreement is just as important as knowing when to stand your ground.

Whatever you do, stay out of arguments via texts or e-mail. Even though you might be trying to "talk" things through electronically, cyber communication can quickly dissolve into ugly and impersonal messages. We're not robots. We need the nonverbal clues that we see on people's faces when we speak with them in person. Without those, texts and e-mail messages are easily misinterpreted. Save your arguments and explanations for a face-to-face meeting.

And by the way, do you know where the phrase "take the high road" came from? Years ago, before modern bridges existed and roads were paved, the roads were level with the ground. Some of them ran through the hills.

It was often faster—more direct—to take the roads across the low ground. But if you took that route, your vehicle would get muddy . . . maybe even stuck.

If you took the high road, the journey would be longer, lonelier, and more difficult, but you would arrive clean.

Take that less-traveled road, following directions that are more positive, diplomatic, and ethical. In the end, you will feel better about yourself.

And you won't get stuck in that nasty mud.

YOU MUST MOVE ON,
BEYOND THE HEARTBREAK

C3 80

You think you've found the love of your life . . . but then, suddenly, they drop the bombshell. They've fallen out of love with you; they need "space"; or, worse yet, they've met someone else. The relationship has run its course. And just like that, he or she is gone. And you're a mess, horribly depressed.

What advice, if any, would you offer someone else going through that same painful heartache? How do you help mend a broken heart?

You're out for a stroll in the park on a beautiful summer day when you see a couple arguing and then breaking up right in front of you. It doesn't matter if it's the man or the woman who storms off. What matters is that, suddenly, one of them is in tears, with no one to turn to. What would you do? When our *WWYD* team proposed this scenario, I had my doubts. I really didn't think anyone would step in and put themselves in the middle of someone else's breakup. But man, was I wrong.

Our hidden cameras started rolling, and one after another,

bystanders stepped in to comfort a complete stranger.

As our heartbroken actress sat alone on a park bench, an elderly woman walked over, put her arm around her, and said, "Maybe you're lucky to get rid of him. What you need to do right now is talk to your best friends and family. Don't text them. Telephone them. Let them hear your voice and you hear their voice."

She walked away with a smile and a wink. "And don't be afraid to tell them what an SOB he was."

When it was the boyfriend who was left behind, sad and dejected, the advice was just as compassionate. This time, it came from a French couple, tourists who reminded us that love and heartache recognize no borders.

"The same thing happened to me two years ago," said Felix Moulin. "I thought I would never find anyone else. For six months I was depressed." But a year after the breakup, he met his new girlfriend, Coline.

"Just like us, one day, when you least expect it," she said in her lovely French accent, "you will meet someone else who will make you forget."

It's the hardest thing to fathom in the midst of heartbreak, but your next great romantic adventure is waiting, right around the corner. It just takes time to get there.

FORGIVENESS

Cʒ ଃ

What would you do if a loved one or best friend refused to forgive you for some misdeed you committed long before? The grudge creates a wedge between the two of you, and your relationship seems like a lost cause.

Anger, bitterness, and vengeance tend to linger. If you allow it to build, it can destroy you with darkness and negativity.

Years ago, I had the pleasure of interviewing actor Will Smith about a new TV show he was producing. From the moment he walked in, I was struck by his positive energy and dynamic personality. His aura engulfed the room like a warm blanket. I had never met anyone quite like him. When I asked him whether he had ever faced envy, jealousy, or betrayal, he smiled broadly and answered, "Sure, haven't we all?"

He quoted lyrics from his rap version of the song "Just the Two of Us," in which he gives advice to his young son: "Throughout life people will make you mad, disrespect you and treat you bad. Let God deal with the things they do, 'cause hate in your heart will consume you, too."

It is absolutely true. The only way for us to live healthy, productive lives is by letting go of hatred and learning to forgive those who have done us harm.

No one knows that better than I do. In the mid-1980s, I fathered a child with a woman to whom I was not married. I lived in Miami and she lived in Canada. We had no plans to get married, but she was determined to give birth and raise the child on her own, which she did.

Julian Michael Quiñones was born on February 12, 1985. I spent time with him, off and on, during the first three years of his life. I paid child support until he was twenty-one years old and had graduated from college. But beyond that, I'm ashamed to say, throughout almost all those formative years, as a father, I wasn't there for Julian.

As a single mom, his mother, in the meantime, did a beautiful, masterful job raising him.

I eventually moved on and married someone else, with whom I have two other children. Yet not a single day went by when I didn't feel the ugly guilt—and pain—of having essentially abandoned my son. Two decades later, while I was going through a divorce, I received a call from Julian's mother. "Your son is now twenty-one years old," she said, "and he really wants to see you." We booked a flight for him to visit me in New York City.

The day he arrived was one of the most exhilarating yet nerve-racking days of my life. I was sweating and shaking like a leaf as I waited for Julian's flight at LaGuardia airport. Suddenly, there he was, bounding off the plane: a tall, incredibly handsome young man with a beaming smile. I gave him a hug and managed to utter, "How in the world can you ever forgive me for not being there for you as a father all these years?"

Without missing a beat, he looked me straight in the eyes and said, "It doesn't matter what has happened in the past. What really matters is what happens from now on."

It was as if, in one fell swoop, he wiped the slate clean and we could start fresh.

We moved in together in New York. And a few months later, after one of his visits to see his mom in Toronto, he returned with a cardboard box.

He placed it in my arms and said, "It's a special gift for you. I've been saving it for a while."

"What is it?" I prodded.

"Just open it."

So I did. And inside the box were dozens and dozens of birthday cards, Father's Day cards, and Christmas cards that Julian had written to me—ever since he was a little boy—but, obviously, had never mailed. Simple, loving, innocent—precious—messages. Some of them included little crayon drawings: a TV box with the stick figure of a reporter holding a microphone.

"To my dad, happy birthday. Love, Julian."

After way too many years, I had finally received my son's good wishes. And I was a bawling mess.

Today, Julian, his brother, Nicco, and sister, Andrea, are not only family; they are best friends. And I am one proud father, happily making up for lost time–thanks to an incredibly loving and impressive young man who chose love over anger and bitterness. He chose to forgive.

WHEN TRAGEDY STRIKES—
THE *CHALLENGER* DISASTER

Cᔆ ᔆↄ

As the father of three children, I cannot fathom the pain and crippling heartache that come with losing a son or a daughter. Imagine the tragedy happening on what was supposed to be the proudest day of your life, as your daughter lifted off from the launch pad at Cape Canaveral, Florida, to become the world's very first schoolteacher in space.

By January 1986, flights aboard America's three space shuttles had become so routine—they would blast off every couple of weeks—that ABC News no longer sent our special science correspondent to cover the liftoffs. The assignments fell on the network's new reporter based in Miami. That was me.

The night before each shuttle launch, I would take a short flight from Miami to Orlando, rent a car, and then drive to Cocoa Beach, Florida, and check into a hotel. It was always fascinating to get a front-row seat and witness these majestic liftoffs.

This particular mission on the space shuttle *Challenger* was special.

Among the seven astronauts who would be blasting off toward the heavens was Christa McAuliffe, a thirty-seven-year-old schoolteacher from Concord, New Hampshire. The bright-eyed social studies teacher and mother of two—who dreamed of leading a class in space—had won the coveted seat over more than 11,500 other candidates.

The morning of January 28 was bitterly cold at the space center, and the launch was delayed by a few hours. Finally, NASA gave *Challenger* the green light.

Christa's parents, Edward and Grace Corrigan, sat in the VIP grandstand, two miles from the launch pad. On a nearby rooftop at mission control headquarters were Christa's husband, Steven, and their nine-year-old son, Scott, and six-year-old daughter, Caroline.

I remember telling my cameraman, David Shannahan, to stay focused on the faces of Christa's mom and dad. If I had any chance of making it on the air on *World News Tonight* that evening, it would be with a story about Christa and perhaps an interview with her proud parents.

There were hundreds of other spectators watching, including the other astronauts' families and friends, NASA workers, and schoolchildren.

The crowd started chanting with the countdown, "Five, four, three, two, one, blast off!"

At exactly 11:37 a.m., *Challenger* lifted off into Florida's crystal-blue skies with schoolchildren yelling, "Go, go, go!" There was wild applause and whistles.

I stood outside our ABC News trailer with a phone to my ear, an open line to our studios in New York.

And then, suddenly, just seventy-three seconds into its flight and five miles into the air, *Challenger* exploded. I watched, stunned—along with millions of Americans seeing it all live on television—as a plume of smoke headed in one direction and another plume turned on itself in a curlicue.

Then came the words I'll never forget, the voice of mission control booming through nearby loudspeakers: "Obviously, a major malfunction."

The crowd was silent. Several children whispered, "What happened?" Silence.

Thirty-three seconds later, the voice came again on the loudspeakers: "We have a report that the vehicle has exploded."

I could hear people screaming, "It didn't explode! How could it explode?"

On the other end of my phone line, a director in New York yelled, "John, you're on the air in twenty seconds. Just tell us what happened."

Of course, I had no idea. At that point, no one did. So I stumbled and stammered, describing, as best I could, what we had just witnessed.

A few minutes later, an ABC technician set up a camera with a live feed to New York. Now I would speak directly to Peter Jennings and the rest of the country.

I was in shock and could barely say much at all. I was choked up, in tears.

During a commercial break, Peter talked to me directly and firmly through my earpiece. "I understand you're shaken by all this," he said. "But you have to get yourself together. Don't let your emotions get the best of you."

Once again, Peter was right. I just needed a little time to catch my breath and absorb the horrific tragedy I had just witnessed.

Later, as I reviewed the footage my cameraman had taken of Christa McAuliffe's parents, I was touched by the transformation on their faces as they had watched the liftoff that morning. They went from utter exhilaration at liftoff . . . to confusion . . . to shock when the mission control voice on the loudspeakers announced, "Obviously, a major malfunction."

Of that moment, her mother, Grace, later said, "I don't think it was that we didn't understand something very horrible had happened. It was the fact that we didn't *want* to believe it."

How does a family carry on after such heart-wrenching tragedy? Christa's mother simply turned to the kind of mission her daughter would have wanted. She's given hundreds of speeches about her daughter and the value of education at schools throughout the country—forty of which now bear Christa McAuliffe's name. She wrote a book about her, *A Journal for Christa*.

And every year she speaks at an Alabama space camp where Teachers of the Year from across the country gather to explore the mysteries of space travel.

"You know why I do it?" she asks with a gentle laugh. "Because Christa would say, 'Hey, Ma, I'm not here. It's a good message. What did I give my life for? I should be there doing it. But I'm not. You can do it.'"

You temper the grief for the loss of your loved one by continuing to share their legacy.

TEACH YOUR CHILDREN WELL

CB BO

In one of my favorite *WWYD* scenarios, we had a parent discipline his or her young son or daughter by forcing them to wear a sandwich board. The child had to stand on a sidewalk with a sign that read I LIED TO MY MOM or I CHEATED ON A SCHOOL TEST or I STOLE SOMETHING AT A STORE. They had to collect five hundred signatures from strangers to make up for their bad behavior.

The idea was to teach the kids a lesson by embarrassing them into changing their ways.

Reactions on the street were equally split. Many passersby applauded the novel approach to discipline. "It'll teach them to never do that again," they told us.

But others—including many parents—argued that it was psychologically damaging to the child.

Child psychologists agree, pointing out that the most effective methods to mold kids are education, mentoring, and conflict-resolution training. "Get tough" approaches, they say, rarely work.

But what if a parent's approach to discipline is much harsher?

What would you do if you witnessed a mom or dad spanking or whipping a child? Would you confront them? Would you rescue the victim? Would you alert the authorities? Or would you not say a word, deciding that a mother or father should be allowed to parent in whatever manner they choose?

It turns out that if you do nothing, you might not raise too many eyebrows. Today in the United States, the only person you can legally hit is a child. Hit your partner and you will be arrested for domestic violence. Hit another adult and you will be charged with assault. But hit a four-year-old child and you can call yourself a "loving parent."

It's an issue that's very close to my heart. When I was a child, I was mischievous, a little troublemaker. As the only boy in the family, I was always fighting with my two sisters. My mother, although very sweet and kind, was also a strict disciplinarian.

Whenever I misbehaved, it wasn't unusual for Maria to enforce that discipline with the threat of corporal punishment. Now and then she would get so angry she would chase me around the house with a broom or a belt, or she would grab a shoe and throw it at me. I really don't think she meant to cause me any serious harm, but there were a few times when I couldn't outrun her and was hit by some flying household missile.

It wasn't all that unusual. That was the way many moms and dads parented in my neighborhood—and in much of the country—back in the 1960s. In an effort to enforce good behavior, they spanked their kids, hit them with a belt or with a switch, which is merely a thin tree limb from the backyard.

They truly believed that if you spared the rod, you spoiled the child.

It happened even in school. At Rhodes Junior High, which I attended—as well as many schools in San Antonio—male teachers, often coaches, had a wooden paddle with which they would strike students on their rear ends.

Some of the more ingenious coaches even drilled holes in their paddles to add speed—and pain—to them. If you were late to class or argued with a teacher or misbehaved in any way, you were sentenced to paddle punishment. And it was terrifying.

It turns out those parents and teachers were horribly wrong. A multitude of studies now show that physical punishment doesn't work for the child, for the parents, or for society. Spanking does not promote good behavior; it contributes to a violent society. Studies show that the more physical punishment a child receives, the more aggressive he or she will become. The more children are spanked, the more likely they will be abusive toward their own children.

Sadly, today many parents still strongly believe in corporal punishment. They spank and hit their children because it's the way they were disciplined themselves. Usually, they do it behind closed doors to ensure no one else is watching or listening.

Take, for example, the case of Adrian Peterson, a star football player for the Minnesota Vikings who was indicted for allegedly brutally hitting his four-year-old son with a switch.

The reason Peterson was charged with a crime was not that he spanked his child, but rather that he hit him too hard. The boy was covered with bruises and welts that broke through his skin. Peterson's lawyer confirmed that his client had spanked his son with a switch, explaining that he was doling out discipline much like "he experienced as a child, growing up in East Texas." His family and friends said Peterson had grown up in a household where his father had used whippings as disciplinary measures.

Peterson himself admitted that he was "not a perfect parent." He added, "But I am, without a doubt, not a child abuser."

As soon as the scandal broke, other football players and celebrities came to Peterson's defense, claiming that physical punishment of a child was all part of "Southern culture." They argued that if spanking a child was against the law, many of their parents and grandparents would be in prison.

The argument is ridiculous. The world has outlawed many reprehensible "norms" that were once considered culturally acceptable.

It is high time we give the most innocent of victims a voice and prosecute all violence against children—not just the kind that leaves them seriously bruised and battered.

After his case made headlines, Adrian Peterson apologized for the hurt he had brought to his son. He later pleaded no contest to recklessly injuring his four-year-old.

As for his method of parenting, Peterson said he was getting psychological counseling "to discuss alternative ways of disciplining a child that may be appropriate."

We can only hope he follows through with it. Because no matter what you call it or why you do it, beating a child is abuse.

And it must be stopped.

THE POWER OF A SMILE AND A KIND WORD

CƷ ℬↄ

When I was a kid, I was infatuated with the world of broadcasting. I would go to sleep listening to my little transistor radio, dreaming of someday delivering music and news to listeners all over south Texas.

Whenever my favorite announcers and disc jockeys would make public appearances at street festivals or openings of new stores, there was twelve-year-old Johnny Q waiting for an autograph and maybe some advice on how to someday break into the business.

Nine times out of ten, they would ignore me, blowing right past my outstretched arm with the pen and paper. I'm sure there was no malicious intent by these local celebrities, but of course my feelings were hurt. The message was that I just wasn't worthy of even a minute of their time.

I vowed right then and there that if I ever made it in broadcasting, I would never do that. And that's why today, whenever *anyone* asks for a picture or an autograph, I'm there, signing and grinning away.

Never underestimate the power of a smile or a kind word. It

doesn't matter how old you are or where you live or what you do for a living. It opens doors, breaks the ice, and warms the heart. It also, quite often, shatters stereotypes.

But we don't do it often enough, because it seems we're always in a rush . . . always in a hurry. There's never enough time to be polite and gracious.

So the minute we jump into that taxi, get in line for our morning coffee, or stand next to a stranger in an elevator, we withdraw into our own little worlds—mesmerized by our smartphones, wired into them by those ubiquitous earbuds.

And too often, when we do make eye contact, we get lazy and quickly size people up, judging them by their outward appearances.

The problem is we're often terribly wrong with those initial impressions.

And you can find out just *how* wrong you are by cracking a smile and offering a friendly greeting to that stranger. Ask them how their day is going; find out where they are from. Do they have a family?

Be *genuinely* interested in your fellow human being. And if either of you is in too much of a rush, just shoot them a smile. There's always time for that. In this hectic, harried—and, yes, sometimes fear-filled—world of ours, we often don't even make eye contact anymore.

I cannot tell you how many times I have reversed the frowns on the faces of grumpy, tired, miserable folks driving a cab, standing at an airline's counter, or sitting behind a glass window at a bank by surprising them with a wink or a funny line. It was almost as if they needed permission to smile again.

You may find that your kind gesture is returned in spades.

Suddenly, you have a better seat on the plane, that surcharge on your credit card is reversed, you're offered an extra drink on the house. Me? I'm just happy with a kind word and a smile in return. Studies show that it stimulates the brain-reward mechanism. It reduces stress and lowers blood pressure and generally makes us feel better.

The more you smile, the longer you live. A recent study of pre-1950s baseball cards of major league players found that the span of each player's smile could actually predict the span of his life. Players who didn't smile in their pictures lived an average of only 72.9 years. Players with beaming smiles lived an average of almost 80 years.

Now there's something to smile about.

WHAT IF IT WAS YOU? WHAT IF IT WAS ME?

❧ ❧

You're walking down a dark alley late at night and, suddenly, you see two big, scary-looking guys walking toward you. They could be harmless. But you quickly assess the situation. You pick up your pace, change directions, hide your wallet or cell phone. You might even grab that can of mace.

You have mentally profiled them, instantly. We *all* do it. It's a biological response, imbedded in our DNA. A matter of survival. Back in our prehistoric caveman and cavewoman days, we had to quickly assess danger and decide whether to fight or flee.

That's why the hair on the backs of our necks still stands up when we sense a threat.

Of course, we no longer live in those caves. And yet that instinct is still there. So, in today's world, when we start judging people, we must stop ourselves and ask, "Why am I presuming the worst of this person?"

It's not easy. A classic example of that was our scenario that asked, what would you do if, while you were on your way to school or work one morning, the person walking in front of you suddenly collapsed? She might have fainted or had a stroke or a heart attack. You don't know.

When the victim was a well-dressed businesswoman, passersby reacted within seconds. They covered her with a coat, fashioned a pillow for her head, and immediately called 911. Very impressive.

We switched actors and found a very different reaction. The fallen victim was then an older homeless man. Dirty, smelly . . . and carrying a can of beer. What a difference in the way folks reacted. When he collapsed, eighty-eight people walked by and no one would stop.

Along came one of the most extraordinary people I've ever met. Her name was Linda Hamilton. She was an African American woman who was walking with a cane because she'd suffered a stroke. As luck would have it, she was homeless herself. She stopped and started asking the crowds of people walking by, "Excuse me, can someone please call an ambulance for this man?" Unbelievably, twenty-six more people walked by, some of them stepping over the man on the ground.

Linda then struggled over to our homeless man, grabbed his can of beer, and dropped it in a trash can. It was an effort to give the man a bit of dignity. Still, no one stopped. Finally, Linda leaned over our victim and whispered in his ear, "My name is Linda. I don't know what your name is, but I'm going to call you Billy. And don't you worry, my man, I'm gonna stay right here until help arrives."

She remained by his side until, finally, a woman stopped and called 911.

When I spoke to Linda later, she told me life had been very hard on her. Two years in a homeless shelter, panhandling, mental illness. But when she saw a man down, she just had to stop and help.

Why? "Because I'm homeless myself. I have walked in that man's shoes," she said. "And because God . . . he gave me a heart."

Thank goodness that, for whatever reason, Linda was put in our path, was caught on our hidden cameras, and stayed around long enough to teach us all a very valuable lesson. Because no one understands the plight of others better than a person who's been there.

IT'S JUST THE RIGHT THING TO DO

Cʒ ঙ

Everyone has been either the victim or the beneficiary of lost money at one point or another.

You're walking down the sidewalk and there it is on the ground: an envelope stuffed with ten one-hundred-dollar bills. A thousand dollars! Maybe some absentminded cashier hands you an extra hundred-dollar bill with your change.

Money from Heaven! It's your lucky day. You start spending the cash in your mind. Time for a little shopping spree.

But do you really want to keep what is not rightfully yours? It says a lot about a person's character. The fact is, once we start cheating on the little stuff, we find it easier to cheat on the bigger stuff.

What if the opposite happens? You're the one who accidentally drops and loses that envelope full of cash. Or you're the cashier who has to pay the missing hundred dollars because you miscounted some customer's change. Time stops. Your heart sinks. How could this have happened to you? You work hard for your money!

We staged our "lost money" scenario right outside a bank. On the sidewalk, we purposely placed a hundred-dollar bill. And we made sure it was paper clipped to a bank statement with someone's name on it. If people found it, they would know exactly to whom it belonged.

Who would try to return the money? Who would keep it?

Sure enough, one man picked up the cash and kept walking. "This is my lucky day," he later told me. "Finders, keepers." Another woman, out shopping with her daughter, also pocketed the cash.

When I caught up with her and explained that the name on the bank statement was mine, she angrily responded, "I'm broke. I'm hungry. Don't play with me. Get out of my goddamn face, bitch!"

I'd never been called that before.

Soon the heroes arrived—a whole parade of people who spotted the money and, without hesitation, walked into the bank. An unemployed man returned the money. A bus driver returned the money. A Chinese food deliveryman returned the money.

We literally could not give away the cash.

Among the Good Samaritans was a Jewish man who scanned the parking lot for someone in distress and then returned the cash at the bank window.

"It's called a mitzvah," he told me. "The commandment that says you should always return something that's lost to its rightful owner. God is watching."

No one touched us as deeply as a disheveled old woman who shuffled down the sidewalk, then stumbled upon the cash. Her name was Simone and she was homeless and unemployed. Every day, she walked two hours to a friend's home for a hot meal, then walked back to a city shelter, where she slept.

She had only seven dollars to her name, but guess what? She stopped, picked up the cash . . . and returned it to the bank.

Through tears, Simone told me, "I have literally nothing in my life, but I will never take someone else's money, because it's just not right."

A little pearl of wisdom from a homeless woman who certainly didn't have much in material possessions but was rich in character.

We should all have that kind of wealth.

EVERY NOW AND THEN BITE YOUR TONGUE

CR ℬ

We have all flown off the handle when we experienced terrible customer service. Your cable box goes out during the big game, and you are on hold *forever* with the cable company before you are connected to a very friendly someone at an offshore call center who just repeats, "Thank you, sir, I will try my best to help you," after verifying for the second time each piece of information you originally entered twenty minutes earlier in response to the cable company's voice-automated requests. Or you are in a rush to zip into and out of the post office, and it is just the opposite. It feels like they are trying to find the cure for cancer in the amount of time it takes them to figure out the right postage for a letter. It is a huge challenge not to become irate and scream at the innocent person trying to help you, "It's JUST. A. STAMP!" Yes, *it's just a stamp.*

At Blues City Café in Memphis, Tennessee, our very sweet yet absentminded waiter, Sean, aimed to take "very good care" of his customers, but when he couldn't get their orders right over and over again, I was very surprised at how patient his customers were. Instead of flipping out, a lovely couple visiting from Australia felt genuinely worried for him. They did not want to cost "the poor bloke" his job even though he ruined their lunch. Their advice: just relax.

Another customer "just rolled with it." After suffering through the lousy service from our waiter, she took matters into her own hands. She wrote down her own table's order, walked over to the kitchen, and delivered it to the chef.

"When you get angry at someone, you are only hurting yourself," she told me. "Make the best of it, and if you can't get what you want, just do it yourself."

Great advice. But today you can rate the service at any business from afar, without ever having to look your server in the eye.

It's called Yelp, the online "urban guide" service that enlightens us with all kinds of reviews as we search for the best hotel, restaurant, nail salon, or even hardware store.

And, of course, the place of business also benefits—when the reviews are positive. It's great publicity.

Conversely, when the customers' assessments are negative, both the businesses and their employees are hurt. And maybe they deserve to be. We should all sound an alert when someone is doing something poorly or just plain wrong.

But what if a bad review was written when the store or one of its employees was simply having an off day?

It may make us feel good to vent our frustrations from our bad experience, but wouldn't it be better to first try to resolve or correct the issue before going for someone's jugular? After all, maybe the business owner is unaware of the problem and totally innocent.

Maybe we shouldn't be so quick to judge when we experience rude, subpar, or just downright bad service.

What *should* you do? Try to give folks the benefit of the doubt. Think about what they might be going through. Maybe your server or attendant is exhausted because they are working two jobs to try to stop an eviction from their home. Or maybe the server's heart is being ripped out by an ugly, contentious divorce. Or a loved one is terribly ill. They are depressed and distracted and would rather be anywhere else than at work. Every now and then, cut people a little slack.

WALKING IN THEIR SHOES

 catch ed ❧

Take a stroll down the street in any major city in America and you will see them: the homeless. Sleeping on our sidewalks, begging for food and money. How often do we take notice and offer a helping hand? How many of us simply try to ignore them and keep walking?

Is it because we don't care? Probably not. Many of us are just afraid of approaching them. Or we presume that they've brought homelessness on themselves with drug use or alcoholism, and we worry that any money we give them might be used to feed their destructive habits.

What if you were sitting at a restaurant and you saw a Good Samaritan bring a beggar in off the street and try to buy him a meal? She gives the bartender twenty dollars and says, "Please give this man whatever he wants."

As soon as the woman leaves, however, the guy behind the counter starts insulting the homeless man. "You're dirty," he says. "You smell. Our customers don't want you in here." He kicks the beggar out and pockets the twenty bucks. That is exactly the scenario we staged at a popular restaurant on Long Island, New York.

The result? Well, sadly, more than a few customers agreed with the bartender. One man told us, "This is the wrong place to feed the homeless." A couple of women complained that the man was filthy and smelled. "He should take his food and eat outside."

Soon, however, we were met with the heroes. First up was Anthony Gambino, a guy who started by making fun of our "bum." "Run him through the dishwasher in the back. And then feed the guy a couple of croutons off the floor," he said, laughing.

But when our bartender tried to keep the cash, Anthony had a change of heart. "You gotta give him his money. Look, none of us really knows what that man has been through." He then ordered some skirt steak tacos for our homeless man . . . and walked outside to hand-deliver them. He even offered him a beer.

"I've been through some hard times in my life," Anthony later told me. "Other people were there for me. I try to do the same thing."

But the greatest inspiration of the day came when, like a vision from Heaven, an older man walked into the restaurant. He was dressed all in white, with gray hair and a white beard. Arnie Gerber sat next to our beggar and offered him his glass of water.

When the bartender started complaining, Arnie raised his voice. "You are wrong. Absolutely wrong. Have you never found yourself in bad shape? Have you never needed help? Have you never had something happen to you that you wish hadn't happened? Or that you wish you could get out of? We don't know what happened to this poor guy!"

You could have heard a pin drop in the restaurant. The noise and the clatter of intolerance were silenced by an old man's simple message: Never judge those who are less fortunate than you. Take a walk in their shoes, and maybe, just maybe . . . you might understand.

UNITE THE WORLD

⌘ ⌘

Have you ever felt embarrassed and frustrated because some wine snob was snickering while you tried to figure out which bottle you'd like with dinner? Or you were ignored by a snooty salesperson at a high-end store who judged your net worth by the gym clothes you were wearing? Or you were forced to wait behind a velvet rope because some obnoxious nightclub doorman decided you didn't measure up to the crowd inside? We've all experienced unkind treatment based on frivolous generalizations and/or expectations.

In our *WWYD* scenario, "Ben" was shopping for a new street look at an urban fashion store. The problem was Ben was white and the store catered to a mostly black and Latino clientele. A salesman not only ridiculed Ben's desire to look "urban chic," but he made it clear Ben wasn't welcome.

The scene reminds me of how my own family was treated at stores in Ohio, where we were farmworkers back in the late sixties. Every weekend, when we'd go shopping for groceries in Toledo, we would encounter the ugly stares of patrons who judged us by our dirty clothes and our funny accents. Often they wouldn't even allow us inside their stores.

Flash forward to our urban store, where a young African American man named Chaz decided to take on our insensitive salesman. "Everybody is going to have their own opinion about how people should dress," he said, "because they might not be able to put it together like we can. I used to feel that way, but no longer. We need to unite the world. You feel me?"

I sure wish we'd had someone like Chaz speak up for my family back in Ohio. It's a powerful reminder that each one of us is our own "chief justice" in the supreme court of life. Even our simplest everyday decisions are based on how we rule on the oral arguments that the rest of the world presents us. If we carefully weigh all those outside opinions and realize that our rulings don't always have to be black or white, we take a small step forward toward uniting the world. Even when that decision is as simple as deciding who wears what.

HERE'S TO THE UNDERDOGS

ᘓ ᘔ

Like so many people who come to the rescue in our *WWYD* scenarios, I always cheer for the underdog. No doubt it's because I was one of them. Nothing was ever handed to me on a silver platter. On the contrary, I was repeatedly told I would never make it. I had to fight tooth and nail for everything I have accomplished. And I'm still fighting.

That's why I love people like Robert Rodriguez. Sure, like me, he's Mexican American, born and raised in my hometown of San Antonio. But here's a guy who knew from a very early age what he would do for the rest of his life. He was eleven years old when his father bought one of the very first videotape recorders, which came with a camera. Robert started shooting films and has never stopped: action movies, sci-fi, horror, drama, stop-action animation.

Today he's one of the most creative and imaginative directors the film industry has ever seen. He's also a screenwriter, producer, cinematographer, editor, musician, and actor. Among his groundbreaking film sagas are: the Mexico Trilogy, *From Dusk Till Dawn*, the Spy Kids franchise, *Sin City*, *Machete*, *The Faculty*, *The Adventures of Sharkboy and Lavagirl in 3-D*, and *Planet Terror*.

He has also launched his own cable-TV channel, El Rey.

But, growing up, Robert had no connection to anyone in the moviemaking business. His father was a salesman, his mother a nurse. Robert was a boy with a dream and not much else. The underdog. His chances of making it in Hollywood were slim to none.

Yet he was known around his neighborhood as the "kid who makes movies." He learned to do all the work himself: camera, lights, sound.

"Someone told me long ago," he said, "that if you're creative and you become technical, you will be unstoppable."

His props were whatever he could find around the house. The setting for his films: the streets of San Antonio. His cast and crew? His nine brothers and sisters. In high school, while kids were writing term papers, Robert would turn in term movies.

"The teachers knew that I would put much more effort into a movie," he said, "than I would into an essay."

A lot of people go to a movie and say, "I can do that." Robert would watch films and announce, "I *will* do that."

It wasn't easy. In the 1980s and '90s, there were very few Hispanics making movies. But, Robert's sister Angela was an actress who moved to New York to try her luck.

He tells the story of how heartbroken his father was when Angela called home one day, saying she was changing her name from Rodriguez to Llamas because she couldn't get work as a Hispanic.

"I remember being very upset—not at my sister, but at an industry that would deny you work simply because of your name," he said. "I became very determined that day that I would never, never change my name."

At the University of Texas, Robert's grades were not good enough for him to get into the school's film program, so he created a daily comic strip that ran in the student newspaper. It was titled *Los Hooligans*, and many of its characters were based on his siblings.

The best writers chronicle what they know. The comic strip was a big success. In the meantime, Robert continued shooting short films, and one of them finally earned him a spot in the UT film program. It was there that Robert's first action movie, *El Mariachi*, became the stuff of legend. He shot it for only seven thousand dollars, money Robert and a buddy raised by taking part in medical research studies.

El Mariachi went on to win the audience award at the Sundance Film Festival.

It was Robert Rodriguez who—for the first time—gave starring roles to Hispanic actors such as Salma Hayek, Antonio Banderas, Danny Trejo, and Cheech Marin. Singlehandedly, he started to change the moviemaking landscape.

Early on, Hollywood resisted. When he first pitched *Spy Kids*, a film that centered on a Latino family, the studios kept asking, "Why does it have to be a *Hispanic* family? Why can't we make them American?"

"Because I based it largely on my family, my own history. It's what I know," he explained. "Besides, they *are* American, just Hispanic Americans." The studios still didn't get it.

And then Robert hit upon the answer. "Look," he said, "you

don't have to be British to like James Bond." Finally, they got it. The studio heads were not necessarily being biased; they just wanted a response they could understand.

"Too often, Hollywood is all about remaking old stories, rebooting old concepts," said Robert. "Meanwhile, Latinos have all the stories that have never been told. Unique and fascinating tales about their world, their culture. And they are universal stories that everyone can relate to.

"Ironically, it's the people who cannot get into the movie business these days who have all the 'gold' in their pockets, all that gold in their *corazón*—their hearts."

Seventeen percent of the American population is Latino—that's 54 million and growing. Yet fewer than five percent of the faces we see on television are Hispanic.

The percentage of Latinos on El Rey, Robert Rodriguez's new cable channel? Sixty percent.

And by the way, if you want to change your Hispanic name to something more "English-sounding," he will not hire you.

The underdog is now calling the shots . . . and changing even more of the media landscape.

TAKE TIME FOR THE MOVED
AND THE SHAKEN

CƷ ℬↃ

We are a nation obsessed with fame and fortune. The richer our celebrities are, the more beautiful, the skinnier, and the more famous, the more we want to be just like them. Material wealth, power, and beauty consume us.

Some of that is okay. We can always dream. But every now and then, we should take measure of exactly what it is we admire in our fellow human beings. If it's merely the fact that they are rich, good-looking, and famous, we need to reassess. Because, let's face it, money and beauty can be fleeting. And how many times have we been disappointed by our all-too-fallible celebrity idols?

I have had the pleasure of interviewing more than my share of famous and wealthy people all over the world.

But as interesting—and sometimes fascinating—as these "movers and shakers" can be, given the choice, I would still much rather speak to the moved and the shaken of this world.

The deepest, most enlightening, and, yes, most rewarding

conversations I've had have been with people who never sought the media spotlight. They have been with the survivors of war, poverty, famine, and natural disasters.

They are the ones who have discovered the truly important things in life, and those aren't fame and fortune. They are perseverance, faith, hard work, and the love of family.

Sure, it's always fun and exciting to meet a star of television or film, someone whose music you love, or even a political leader whom you admire and support. But celebrities, by the very nature of their fame, get more than their share of recognition. Sometimes it's almost like they are famous for being famous.

I would much rather give a voice to those people who have none. Like the children who live in the sewers of Bogotá, Colombia. Or the dwindling native tribes of the Yanomami in the Amazon. Or the Penan in Borneo, the world's last nomadic tribe.

I have spent time with the Haitian slave children in the sugarcane fields of the Dominican Republic, and with the Pygmy natives of the Congo. I have witnessed true strength of character and the spirit to survive.

When journalism is done right, we should be telling more of their stories.

If ever you have the chance, take a listen. You might well discover a new hero, a new idol. And it will have nothing to do with money, beauty, or fame.

DON'T RUSH THROUGH LIFE!
TIME TO UNPLUG

CB BO

One of the most memorable *What Would You Do?* scenarios we've filmed featured a businessman at lunch blabbing away, non-stop, on his cell phone. He was so loud he totally disrupted the dining experience for the rest of the guests. Time and again he was confronted by other diners. Several of them had our loudmouthed actor kicked out of the restaurant.

The scenario would be funny if it wasn't so true. Cell phones have become a kind of appendage. We're addicted to them.

My father, Bruno, was amazed at the crazed, hectic life that I lead as a television reporter. He was also disturbed by this little device that seemed glued to my hand.

"Son, you're always running at warp speed," he would tell me. "You really need to slow down." He was a man whose main job as a janitor was to sweep and mop the floors at my old high school. He always took time to talk—face-to-face—with the teachers and students who grew to love him.

At home, he loved to listen to music, dance, and tend his gardens. He took time—lots of it—to quite literally smell the roses. He didn't own a cell phone until the last few years of his life—and then used it only for emergencies. He lived into his early nineties. I think he was on to something.

Maybe it's time we take one day out of the week to disconnect from our busy lives. Power off those cell phones and laptops. Call it Sunday (or any other day) Unplugged.

Instead of constantly checking little screens for texts and e-mails, we can create other, much more rewarding rituals. We can relearn to appreciate the natural beauty that surrounds us and have deeper conversations with our loved ones, face-to-face.

A wonderful lesson from Bruno. He spent nearly a century on Earth and died a happy and serene man.

ALWAYS STAY CURIOUS

Cʒ ℘

Back in school, I was the kid who would always raise his hand when the teacher asked, "Are there any more questions?"

It didn't matter that it was the end of the school day and that every other student was itching to go home. I was curious, inquisitive, always with a hungry mind. No wonder my classmates would let out a collective groan.

I have what experts call a "high curiosity quotient." People with that kind of "CQ" find novelty exciting and are quickly bored with routine. They tend to be nonconformists and generate unique, original ideas.

There's no doubt in my mind it was that deep-seated curiosity—my yearning to travel to faraway places and willingness to challenge conventional thinking—that eventually got me a correspondent's position at ABC News, launching me on this fascinating odyssey.

One of the highlights: my two-week adventure with the awesomely fascinating Jane Goodall in Tanzania, Africa.

She is a woman who epitomizes the power of the curious mind.

We camped out at Gombe Stream National Park along the shores of Lake Tanganyika. Every night, I was mesmerized—and, yes, a tad scared—by the sounds of lions, leopards, and elephants hunting and grazing just outside our tents.

Gombe is the protected preserve where Jane Goodall spent more than thirty years studying chimpanzees in the wild—much of that time, all by herself. Just watching, documenting.

She had no formal training in animal psychology, but her research was groundbreaking.

She was the first to document that chimpanzees could fashion and use tools to feed themselves. She discovered that they were not strictly vegetarian and could also be violent and aggressive—even cannibalistic. She also found that chimps have unique and individual personalities and are capable of rational thought and emotions, like joy and sorrow.

Hiking with Jane Goodall through the very same forest where she conducted all her research, I was blown away. Unlike others, she didn't simply assign numbers to her subjects; she gave them names. And I got to meet them face-to-face. There were Atlas, Fifi, Frodo, Gimble, and the alpha male, Freud—furry friends whose genes are more than 99 percent the same as ours.

"The chimps help us realize," Jane said to me, "that we are part of the natural world, that we have a special relationship with the other nonhuman animals with whom we share this planet."

Thanks to her curious, inquisitive mind, Jane Goodall revolutionized the study of animals. It's as if she has handed us an ancient looking glass through which we can meet an ancestor.

Be like Jane. Keep learning. Keep exploring. Stay curious.

You don't actually have to find all the answers. It's about relishing the unknown and the uncertainties. It's all about the journey.

DO SOMETHING!

CB 80

The reverend Martin Luther King Jr. once eloquently said, "Our lives begin to end the day we become silent about things that matter." That pretty much explains the whole concept behind *What Would You Do?*

Every day, every one of us witnesses something that matters—if not to us, then to our fellow man or woman. What do we do when we see or hear something disturbing—someone in need or in trouble, or someone being ridiculed—and that little voice in the back of our head says, "Do something"? Do we speak up and sound an alarm? Or do we remain silent, choosing to mind our own business?

Staying quiet and walking away is certainly the easier, safer way out. We avoid being delayed or inconvenienced. We are spared from the threat of becoming targets ourselves. And we're not perceived as a "rat" or a troublemaker.

But every time we keep to ourselves individually, we lose something as a society. By refusing to get involved and put an end to the wrongdoing, we wind up perpetuating pain and injustice.

Of course, at *WWYD*, we never suggest that bystanders become *physically* involved in any situation that might seem disturbing. Sometimes our effort to jump in and help can backfire. That's why, in our hidden camera scenarios, we always have plainclothes security standing by, very close to the action. If the scene becomes too heated—and I can't get there soon enough—our off-duty officer steps in and stops the action.

Instead of angrily confronting the protagonist, we can also simply ask, "Is everything okay here?" Or we can call 911 from a safe distance, alert the authorities, and get help.

That's when something truly impressive happens. Once someone raises his or her voice or lends a helping hand, it's like society is given a breath of fresh air. A brave soul steps up, and suddenly, other people join in. It's almost as if the rest of us were waiting for permission to speak up. The thief, the racist, the cheater, or the bully is singled out and exposed for what he is. Younger, more innocent bystanders are taught a lesson or two about standing up to evil.

And we are all the better for it.

After filming more than four hundred different *WWYD* scenarios, I can't go anywhere without people asking me, "Do you think America is becoming more or less tolerant of different races, cultures, and lifestyles?"

I think we have generally become a much more tolerant melting pot. The fact is the very face of this nation is now changing before our eyes. This is, after all, a country where minorities will be the majority by the year 2043. We were once a black and white country. Now we are a rainbow.

The latest study and poll by the Pew Research Center bears this out. We have little choice but to get along.

By overwhelming majority, respondents said they were fine accepting people of other races into their families. Fifty-three percent of Americans said they support same-sex marriage (up twenty-one percent in just ten years).

The only areas where Americans are *not* more tolerant is in their attitudes toward Muslims, atheists, and illegal immigrants. Negative responses toward Muslims have spiked as high as sixty-three percent in recent years. No doubt this is spurred by the terrorist attacks of 9/11, the 2013 Boston Marathon, and, more recently, the horrific slayings of hostages by ISIS.

Half of all respondents said they do not want an in-law who doesn't believe in God. Forty-five percent of Americans see the deportation of undocumented workers as a "good" thing. Clearly, we have a way to go toward acceptance and tolerance.

As a lifelong journalist and now the host of *WWYD*, I have observed, studied, and learned much about human nature, both the good and the bad.

I've had chills run down my spine as assassins for Central American death squads explained in excruciating detail why they killed people for their politics.

I have sat misty-eyed as the man who pulled children out of Colombian sewers explained why he simply could not sleep at night knowing that kids lived in such misery.

WWYD has shown us that there are good people out there, everywhere. They always outnumber the bad. It's just that sometimes they are a silent majority.

The issues and scenarios we tackle on *WWYD* happen every day, all over the world, but they usually happen in the shadows. *WWYD* has brought them into the light.

And the response has been phenomenal. Millions of viewers tune in every week, and thanks to the Internet, tens of millions more all over the world watch our scenarios online. I constantly receive tweets and e-mails from viewers everywhere, from Great Britain to Australia, from Istanbul to China . . . viewers pleading for us to bring *WWYD*'s hidden cameras to their countries.

Of course, the show has also made it impossible for me to enjoy a quiet dinner at any restaurant or board an airplane without people approaching me and asking, "Okay, John, what's about to happen now?" I cannot walk down the street without people stopping me and thanking me for putting the show on the air.

But do you know what's truly impressive? Knowing that teachers in high schools and professors in colleges and universities throughout the country now use recordings of our scenarios as teaching tools in psychology and sociology classes.

It is also heartwarming to hear from so many families who tell me they watch our hidden-camera scenarios together—parents and their children, watching together and then discussing what they would do in a particular situation.

WWYD has clearly touched a nerve with viewers. Many times when we're filming a segment and I approach bystanders who have done something incredibly admirable, they tell me they did so because they've watched the show and promised themselves—or their children—that the next time they faced an ethical dilemma, they would do the right thing.

So maybe the world would indeed be a better place if we all behaved as if we were on *WWYD?*. We might well be on our best behavior.

Short of that, we can learn valuable lessons about tolerance, ethics, and morals from everyday *WWYD* heroes like that American serviceman we met while shooting a scenario in the town of Kingston, New York.

The scene we set was simple. A man walked into a deli, and when he noticed that the server behind the counter was a Muslim wearing a taqiyah, the traditional Muslim prayer cap, he refused to buy his lunch from him.

"You're a terrorist," he told his server. "I don't forget 9-1-1. Your people—Muslims—did that!"

Most customers refused to get involved. A few stood up for the Muslim attendant. And one of the deli's patrons actually agreed with our bigoted actor. As we wrapped the shoot for the day, in walked an American soldier in uniform. We had no idea how he would react.

As soon as he heard our bigoted actor's rants, he spoke up, clearly and precisely.

"We live in America," he said after ordering his lunch. "He can practice any religion he wants."

Our angry racist kept pushing. "Aren't these guys the enemy? Aren't you fighting against them in Iraq and Afghanistan?"

"Not at the moment," said the soldier. "Right now, I'm only ordering a sandwich."

"Well, I don't think he should be working here."

The soldier's face turned red with anger. "Get out! Put those chips down and go buy your stuff somewhere else. You have a choice to shop anywhere—just like this man has a choice to practice whatever religion he wants. That's the reason I wear the uniform. So anyone can live free in this country."

"Are you a hero?" I asked him after we had explained the that scenario was all part of the show.

"No, sir," he said adamantly. "Heroes come in many shapes and sizes. But that wasn't heroic at all. That was just me, one person, standing up for someone else."

It was so simple and yet so eloquent.

I looked around the restaurant and every single person was beaming with pride.

The next time you witness something disturbing and that little voice inside your head says, 'Do something,' remember the words of that American soldier—or the actions of Linda Hamilton, the African American woman who stopped to help a homeless man when no one else would. They sounded an alarm and lent a helping hand—not because the payback would be a place to live, some reward money, or glory on national TV.

They stopped and helped their fellow man because, as we say in Spanish, their *corazones*, their hearts, told them it was the right thing to do.

What would *you* do?